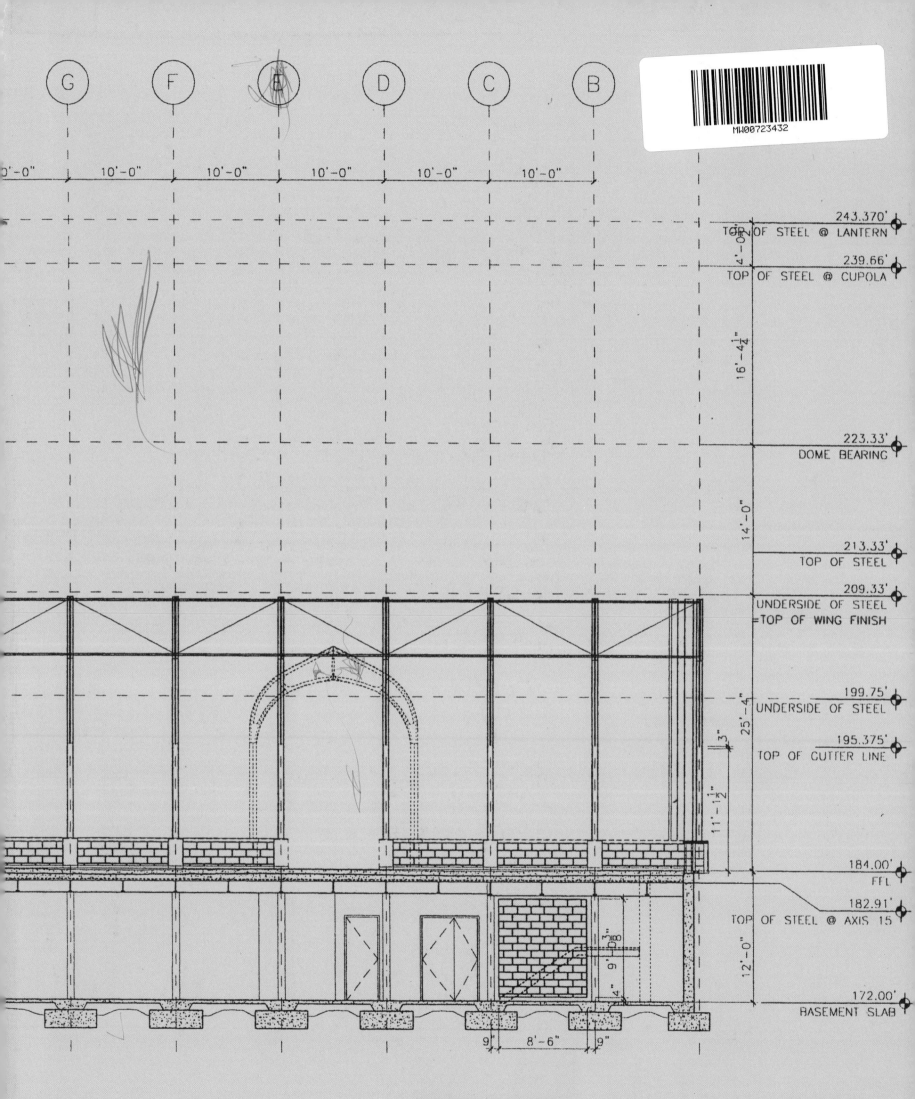

G　　F　　E　　D　　C　　B

0'-0"　　10'-0"　　10'-0"　　10'-0"　　10'-0"　　10'-0"

243.370'
TOP OF STEEL @ LANTERN

239.66'
TOP OF STEEL @ CUPOLA

16'-4¼"

223.33'
DOME BEARING

14'-0"

213.33'
TOP OF STEEL

209.33'
UNDERSIDE OF STEEL
=TOP OF WING FINISH

199.75'
UNDERSIDE OF STEEL

195.375'
TOP OF GUTTER LINE

3"

25'-4"

11'-1½"

184.00'
FFL

182.91'
TOP OF STEEL @ AXIS 15

12'-0"

9'-3⅛"

4"

172.00'
BASEMENT SLAB

9"　　8'-6"　　9"

SECTION B-B CENTRAL DOME

NOT TO SCALE

ELEVATING
THE HUMAN SPIRIT

THE ARCHITECTURE OF GLAVÉ & HOLMES

ELEVATING THE HUMAN SPIRIT

THE ARCHITECTURE OF GLAVÉ & HOLMES

H. RANDOLPH HOLMES, JR.

with HENRIKA DYCK TAYLOR

2019

ROBERT J. PARISE, AIA
Principal & Director, Higher Education Studio

H. RANDOLPH HOLMES, JR., AIA
Senior Principal & President

LORI GARRETT, FAIA
Senior Principal & Director, Higher Education Studio

NEIL WALLS, AIA
Senior Associate & Director of Technology

S. JEANNE LeFEVER, AIA
Principal & Director of Human Resources & Operations

CRYSTAL NEWMAN-JONES
Senior Associate & Director of Marketing

ANDREW B. MOORE, AIA
Principal & Director, Urban Architecture Studio

ELEANOR BARTON, ASID, CID
Former Principal & Director, Interior Design Studio

STEVEN BLASHFIELD, AIA
Principal & Director, Cultural Studio

WINNIE MA SUNG, AIA
Senior Associate & Director of Quality

ROBERT BRYANT
Chief Financial Officer

— CONTENTS —

JAMES MILLARD GLAVÉ
1933 - 2005

This book is dedicated to James Millard Glavé, who served the firm until
his death in 2005. Known as Jimmy to his Ashland grade school buddies
and as Jim to everyone else, his devotion to the firm, the practice of
architecture, and the preservation of great buildings in Richmond and the
Southeast continue to inspire and instruct us. His words and deeds are
with us as we seek to continue and expand upon his legacy.

To Jim and his fellow founders of the firm—William C. Newman and
Samuel A. "Pete" Anderson—we thank you from the bottoms of our
hearts for the leadership you demonstrated. The principles you modeled
underpin the firm's ongoing evolution.

WHEN INVITED TO WRITE THIS FOREWORD I had to ask myself what sets Glavé & Holmes Architecture apart from most other firms. Perusing the images in the following pages we realize the buildings are all very new, but we could easily believe many have been there for a long time. Is that the impression new works are supposed to convey? Isn't new architecture supposed to reflect the progressiveness of the present or be a herald of a dynamic future? Aren't architects obliged to express forward-looking creativity unconstrained by a timeworn past? Indeed, that is what many contemporary practitioners, academics, and pundits tell us we must believe or risk condemnation and ridicule. Even so, no such design laws exist.

Why then should there be any constraint against designing new buildings informed by a historic vocabulary, one that builds on past cultures and engages the wisdom of experience such as in the projects designed by Glavé & Holmes? To answer this question, we need to consider some history. With the end of World War I, most of Europe experienced cultural exhaustion, seen in the demise of a lifestyle enjoyed by established patrician classes. Their way of life was largely defined by their architecture—elegant buildings celebrated with rich trappings of past eras. Such designs were considered no longer appropriate for a new age. Thus was conceived the "International Style," a system of design that eschewed any hint of historic tradition or national identity. The advocates of this radical architectural concept, also dubbed the "Modernist Movement," drew inspiration from new technologies: from factories, machines, ships, automobiles, and other mechanical forms. The new approach shunned any aristocratic pretense and saw its future best expressed in such projects as high-rise public housing and industrial complexes—programs related to working classes.

The United States by contrast experienced minimal disruption from the war and thus was slow to adopt this Modernist stance. Most American firms continued to build happily in traditional modes. Their use of historic styles in the 1920s and '30s added perspective and character to our young cities and new neighborhoods. Indeed, the period produced much informed, high-quality work. World War II, however, reversed this trend. Our haste towards victory taught us how to build functional structures of all kinds quickly and efficiently, devoid of unnecessary frills. This design method was spurred by a handful of leading proponents of Modernism who immigrated to this country to avoid Nazi harassment. Most conspicuous among them were Marcel Breuer, Walter Gropius, and Mies van der Rohe. They were welcomed into America's academe where they attracted many disciples who successfully purged American architecture schools of any teaching of classical and traditional design. Much of this new approach was grounded in the writings and theories of Swiss architect, Le Corbusier, who advocated a complete break from the past.

It must be said that some admirable Modernist works got built here, buildings with glass walls that stood shiningly apart from heavily ornamented and often grimy older structures. Unfortunately, cutting-edge works such as the Seagram Building and Lever House gave architects of lesser talent license to produce quantities of boring, uninspired minimalist designs of their own, resulting in cityscapes diluted of visual character and identity. Also, the Modernists' love of exposed concrete morphed into a style termed "Brutalism," a design ethic characterized by a hard, confrontational aesthetic. Brutalism was particularly favored by institutions, especially museums and universities whose governing bodies wanted to project forward-looking thinking. Contrast, not context, was the priority of the proponents of Brutalism. Their schemes consciously imposed jarring contrast onto otherwise genteel settings.

The Modernists were steadfast in their belief that their designs were beyond reproach because they adhered to scientific theories and thus were endowed with an *intellectual* beauty. But did their buildings also stir up a heartfelt *emotional* beauty? In fact, many people, both educated and otherwise, experienced little feeling of heartfelt beauty from of works of Modernism, especially Brutalism. Nevertheless, most were reluctant to admit any derision towards Modernism for fear of being regarded as culturally naïve. Interestingly, such unspoken disdain revealed itself in a telling way: most Americans continued to live in or build traditional-style homes. Full-blown Modernist single-family houses are exceedingly rare. Even more telling was the fact that many developers saw that housing estates, shopping centers, and office complexes with a traditional look sold well. Bottom-line: the public identified with and drew comfort from familiar historic character even though much of such commercial development demonstrated little fluency in traditional modes.

It was against this background that Glavé & Holmes Architecture undertook a new direction in its practice. Although the firm had its beginnings a half-century earlier, it wasn't until recent years, under the guidance of Senior Partner and President Randy Holmes, that Glavé & Holmes set its focus on the production of traditional, and especially classical designs. Holmes recognized the existence of a healthy market for high-quality traditional and classical work and noted that few firms either in Virginia or elsewhere specialized in it. This new emphasis was nurtured early on by Professor Peter Hodson, a former faculty member of England's University of Portsmouth School of Architecture, who taught summer school courses in the classical language at Richmond's Virginia Commonwealth University (VCU).

Hodson's popular class attracted the interest of Glavé & Holmes staff members and ultimately Holmes himself. He subsequently decided to lead the way toward having his firm become proficient in the classical language and to use its principles of harmony, unity, balance, and stability to lend timeless dignity and appeal to the firm's output. Even so, it was apparent to Holmes that many of his new hires, although talented designers, lacked formal education in classical design.

Aware of what was being offered at VCU, Holmes engaged Professor Hodson to deliver direct instruction to the Glavé & Holmes staff, which led to regular in-house tutoring in the firm's studios during the summer months. To achieve necessary competence, every participant was required to draw the classical orders and to execute a design incorporating them. Hodson's tutorials were supplemented with office lectures by Professor Bill Westfall and by me on the background and fine points of classical design and traditional urban planning.

In this way Glavé & Holmes Architecture took on the challenge of and responsibility for maintaining and extending the relevance for contemporary design in what has been called the "Mother Tongue" of the architecture of Western Civilization: the classical language of architecture. This proactive approach afforded the Glavé & Holmes team the specialized education they were unable to obtain in their standard university curriculum. While still, as a firm, involved in a learning curve regarding the refinements and nuance of this language, they are nonetheless producing works that demonstrate contextual sensitivities and timeless prose. The success of this effort is seen in the multiple works of architecture, planning, and interior design presented in this book.

CALDER LOTH
Senior Architectural Historian
Virginia Department of Historic Resources

— INTRODUCTION —

T HE IDEA FOR THIS BOOK emerged several years ago as the firm was approaching its 50th anniversary. The concept was to commemorate a half-century of architectural service by creating a collection of the firm's works. While I generally supported the idea, admonitions from my childhood about "tooting one's own horn" concerned me. I also thought it reasonable to ask, "Do we really need another book showcasing a firm's portfolio?" But because I have been blessed to be involved with Glavé & Holmes Architecture for a quarter of a century, half of that time in a leadership role, I have thought diligently about the motives behind this particular project.

I am proud of our portfolio and very glad we pursued presenting it in this book. The real intention of the publication is to honor those who laid a solid foundation for the firm long before my arrival and to salute those who are currently guiding and shaping this firm to be an influence in the evolution of the practice of architecture today and in the years to come. I am personally motivated by the recognition that our firm operates from a set of principles that, while similar to other architectural firms, also has distinctions that are noteworthy and ought to be shared. The projects within this book are presented by typology and are evidence of these principles, not only because they are interesting works of built architecture, but because they represent in a concrete way the correlation between abstract principles and design realities.

Honoring the past, saluting the present, and speaking to the future in the context of our work seem to be the right objectives for such a book. I believe it has something to say. It is our goal to do so with grace and humility and to express above all else, a deep appreciation for the firm's many opportunities to serve our clients and our profession.

HONORING THE PAST

Nanos Gigantum Humeris Insidentes
—Bernard of Chartres

THIS PHRASE, WHICH TRANSLATES TO "dwarfs standing on the shoulders of giants," is attributed to Bernard of
Chartres, a twelfth century philosopher and theologian. It truly captures the sense of what we inherited from the
firm's founders, Jim Glavé, Bill Newman, and Pete Anderson.

The firm began in 1965 as Glavé Newman and became Glavé Newman Anderson in 1969. Certain fundamental practices were woven into the culture of the firm and remain at the root of Glavé & Holmes today. They are
stewardship, contextual responsibility, attention to the client, and adaptive reuse of interesting buildings and elements of history. These practices and a shared passion for innovation and insightful thinking were brought to bear
by the founders—and the team they hired—in their early commissions. At that time, firms such as Baskervill & Son
or Marcellus Wright had longstanding prominence in the City of Richmond and Glavé Newman Anderson was the
new kid on the block. So began our assent, bolstered by tenaciousness, strong values, and plenty of good fortune.

My first and deepest appreciation for our founding giants is simply to have been hired in the first place.
When I was looking for work in Richmond in 1990, the firm and the architectural/engineering community was
in the throes of a recession—a recurring headache that firms lasting 50 years or more must inevitably endure.
Like most firms at that time, Glavé Newman Anderson had little work and was struggling. My interviews at
numerous firms in Virginia resulted in the common refrain, "You have an interesting portfolio, but unfortunately we don't have any work." When I applied to Glavé Newman Anderson, it was fortuitous that Bland Wade,
with whom I had worked at Jaquelin Robertson's firm in Charlottesville, was there and supported my applica-
tion. Jim Glavé in particular took the gamble of hiring me, based in part on one wealthy client's decision to
pursue a project in spite of—or perhaps because of—the sagging economy.

The spirit of taking calculated risk against conventional wisdom has encouraged me, as well as other
leaders of the firm, to consider similar steps. The founders and many others including Will Scribner, Bob
Boynton, Dick Ford, William Hubbard, Becky Messer, and David Rau laid the philosophical cornerstone for the
firm. I was entrusted with carrying it forward; a challenge that both fortifies and intimidates me. Their exemplary
sacrifices, hard work, creative energy, and visionary leadership prepared a clear path to follow. Today, the
leadership team and I are committed to honoring our firm's past by being good stewards while we are here and
are determined to leave it better than we found it when we go.

SALUTING THE PRESENT

I know the price of success: dedication, hard work, and
an unremitting devotion to the things you want to see happen.
—Frank Lloyd Wright

REFLECTING UPON THE FIRM'S CURRENT STATUS and recent history gives rise to feelings of extreme gratitude for the group of leaders and designers who have done so much to allow Glavé & Holmes Architecture to serve our generation. Their contributions and outcomes bring to mind Paul Goldberger who advocates for building designs that "challenge and comfort." I believe that our designs address their surroundings contextually and pragmatically in ways that are appropriate, commodious, and exhibit a sense of inevitability and belonging. At the same time, our work embodies the spirit of challenge, pushing the edges of expectation to the point of "WOW" and "Wait a minute, I want to look more closely at this."

Part of the reason for this comes from the firm's commitment to the integration of architecture, interior design, and landscape architecture that is carefully considered for each project. From the early decades of the firm's establishment, there have been both architects and interior designers working side by side. Since I came to the firm there has been a dedicated interior design studio, rather than a few interior designers embedded within architectural studios. Glavé & Holmes interiors go the extra mile to create, when possible, custom designs for lighting, carpets, floor designs, furniture and whatever else is required to support the project's architectural character. Firm leaders recognize that the making of beautiful spaces is more successful when the elements that occupy a room and lend function to it also demonstrate the same design principles that inform the architecture of the room.

This concept extends to a building's surrounding landscape. Great buildings are almost always a composition of both architecture and landscape—a dialogue between the influences a building exerts upon a place and the place's influence upon the building's composition and arrangements. We are determined to go beyond merely recognizing these timeless principles—we want to explore the possibilities that knit these elements into one comprehensive whole.

This process is only truly possible when those working on the design show tremendous respect for the efforts and thinking of the other disciplines involved and work together in a spirit of collaboration. I have witnessed, time and time again, people of deep convictions debating how best to make the intimate correlation between disciplines serve both the client and the place a design will inhabit.

And this *esprit de corps* extends beyond project goals. The firm's leadership exhibits these same principles of reason and unity of purpose when designing the firm's strategic direction and the day-to-day management toward those strategic goals. We see that designing a firm for the future may be one of the greatest design opportunities and challenges our leadership faces. Key among those challenges is the powerful impact technology is having upon the creative process—changes both beneficial and yet daunting to grasp and manage. Architects can become consumed by "virtual building" with its high levels of resolution, detail, and 3D. These exciting tools, however, develop reliance upon a design process that embraces computer "short-cuts" and pre-arranged design solutions to craft buildings that exhibit the latest trends and fads in design. To this challenge, we have intentionally chosen to resist certain tides of "progress." Our leadership team promotes and teaches sketching, watercolor rendering, and still draws on the boards to retain the value of hand-eye coordination for design. In this and other ways, we are committed to the maintenance of certain practices and ways of thinking that are uncommon among many of our contemporary firms.

SPEAKING TO THE FUTURE

Architecture is an expression of values.

—Norman Foster

INTO THIS RAPIDLY CHANGING and technologically revolutionary age of architecture, it is formidable to establish a clear sense of direction and purpose for a design firm. Prognosticators and visionaries disagree as to where the future is leading and what it will hold. For us at Glavé & Holmes, one thing is certain. It is people, the human condition that will establish meaning and value to the advancements that progress brings. And this reality establishes for us a primary reason to practice architecture and to face the future—because we firmly believe that architecture can and should *elevate the human spirit*.

At a conference in Hawaii several years ago, I heard a neurologist speak about humans in the age of rapidly changing technologies. A major point was that while the environment that we exist in has changed dramatically and the rate of change is increasing at unprecedented speed, the human brain has not evolved significantly since the establishment of western culture. We as people can only process the breathtakingly changing world with limited human abilities and consistently depend upon certain basic qualities of life in order to achieve a sense of satisfaction or happiness.

With this in mind, we believe that whatever the future holds for us, we want to create spaces and places imbued with those fundamental and timeless qualities of harmony, rhythm, proportion and human scale that evoke appreciation and a sense of enjoyment. Foremost, we want to make places that clearly respond to prescribed needs and intentions. But commodious and functional architecture may or may not address the basic human need for Beauty. It is to this aspiration for Beauty that we, as a firm, strive tirelessly to understand and conjure in each of our designs. What is Beauty? How do we create it? This is what shines the light on our future path and explorations.

I think that C.S. Lewis was correct in saying that progress means getting nearer to the place you want to be. And if you have taken a wrong turn, then to go forward does not get you any nearer. He writes, "If you are on the wrong road, progress means doing an about turn and walking back to the right road; and in that case, the man who turns back soonest is the most progressive man."

At Glavé & Holmes, we believe progress depends upon embracing time-honored principles. This belief is founded in an appreciation for much of our architectural past, from which valuable lessons and principles can be appropriately applied to craft environments that people find enjoyable and inspiring. Our focus on the human spirit and how to affect it—to have, in the words of Max DePree, a "voice and touch" in the creation of places for human interaction—is where we seek to go as a firm. It necessitates the understanding of western architecture's foundations and so we operate a Summer Classical Institute within our firm to edify our practitioners. We owe immeasurable debt to Peter Hodson, Calder Loth, and Bill Westfall for their contributions in teaching and mentoring members of our firm.

Our path forward also involves the development of critical analysis and thinking about design and its context. We are fortunate to have within the firm's leadership and staff a strong bench of inquisitive learners and insightful minds.

Progress also involves faith—deep convictions that the practices of architecture, interior design, landscape design, planning, and related services exist not as ends unto themselves, but rather as means to an end. As Norman Foster wrote: "Architecture is an expression of values." And for us, it is our values that establish the need for architecture that in turn, in the words of Christopher Wren, "aims at eternity."

More than ever, we need places of Beauty that allow the best of human progress to flourish. Places that serve humanity with innovations that speak creatively to the heart of their needs. Places that challenge us to see ourselves not as who we are, but who we can become. Places that inspire us and elevate the human condition. These goals are aspired to and obtained by our architectural pursuit.

This is our future. Where else should we strive to go?

H. Randolph Holmes, Jr.

GLAVÉ & HOLMES ARCHITECTURE attends to their clients via studios dedicated to each of the firm's market sectors: Higher Education, Cultural, Civic, Hospitality, and Residential. The Interiors Studio works closely with all the others to achieve unified projects inside and out. In the pages that follow, images and descriptions of built work depict the core values of the firm: Exemplary service to the client; contributing positively to each project's physical, cultural, and historical contexts; and serving every project's surrounding communities for the long-term. Glavé & Holmes hopes that their work inspires the practice of architecture in a particular way so that architecture continues to elevate the spirit and challenge mankind to be and do its best.

ACADEMIA

— ENHANCING COMMUNITIES OF LEARNING —

OVER THE YEARS, GLAVÉ & HOLMES Architecture has had the opportunity to add new structures or revitalize buildings at university and private campus settings alike. Historic rehabilitation has long been a calling card for the firm beginning with revered institutions in Richmond during seminal work in the 1970s—at Virginia Commonwealth University, Union Presbyterian Seminary, and the Valentine Museum among others.

In 2003, Glavé & Holmes underwent a structural reorganization and partner and owner Lori Garrett established the Higher Education Studio. During the recession years that followed (2007-12), steady campus work saw the firm through and with a burgeoning of projects it became necessary to have two studios of 8-12 people working on Higher Education projects alone. Since then, Glavé & Holmes has become nationally recognized as leaders in campus architecture and design with established specialties in revitalization of heritage buildings, admissions and campus hospitality facilities, and schools of business. As a result of the firm's renowned expertise, new commissions are emerging beyond Virginia throughout the eastern seaboard.

Critical to Glavé & Holmes' success is its focus on contextual identity—the philosophical and cultural character of a school as well as its physical setting. Discoveries pave the way and become examples for developing new functionality. Whether establishing growth with precinct planning, revising a master plan, or rehabilitating a single building, the goal remains the same: to connect, enhance, and support the existing academic and neighboring communities. Serving the long term is meaningful and to that end, Glavé & Holmes infuses the character of buildings and campuses with new life so that they can be used and loved for decades to come.

Today, following significant growth of the firm since the start of the new millennium, campus commissions comprise more than half of the firm's work. Leadership under Randy Holmes, Lori Garrett, and many others has taken campus architecture and planning to a whole other level as is evidenced from the work at Christopher Newport—which has essentially created a new university from the ground up—to the development of buildings on historic campuses at the University of Richmond, University of Virginia, Washington and Lee University, William & Mary, and Virginia Tech. These outcomes, which are illustrated in the following pages, support learning and creativity while elevating the human spirit at the aesthetic level, the community level, and the civic level.

CHRISTOPHER NEWPORT
UNIVERSITY

— NEWPORT NEWS, VIRGINIA —

OPPOSITE
View of Christopher Newport University's Great Lawn, looking west

OPPOSITE BELOW
Christopher Newport University Campus Plan

OVERLEAF
Christopher Newport Hall, Great Lawn view

GLAVÉ & HOLMES ARCHITECTURE began its long-term relationship with Christopher Newport University in 2006. The firm's initial master site plan for the university has guided a complete transformation of the 260-acre campus beginning with the creation of a centralized Great Lawn framed by new buildings, many designed by Glavé & Holmes. Concurrent with the development of the Great Lawn, numerous other projects envisioned in the Master Plan have been completed or are ongoing.

Integral to the success of the plan is the establishment and execution of the campus' Neo-Classical style: civic in scale yet appropriate to collegiate life. Proportional façades with colonnaded pavilions demark primary entries using classical orders from Tuscan to Corinthian. Primary materials include the campus standard brick with pilasters, cornice work, and pediments of precast concrete. Surrounding the campus green are core buildings that promote student life and welfare and together render an uplifting identity for the university. The following pages present the completed academic and administrative buildings, various types of new student housing—residence halls and a Greek Village— a university chapel and campanile, a student success center, and the expanded recreation and fitness center. Each individual design within the plan elevates the overall aesthetic character of the campus and raises the quality of all the facilities to an exceptional level. Glavé & Holmes collaborated with the Atlanta-based firm of Lord Aeck Sargent on the Lewis Archer McMurran, Jr. Hall, Mary Brock Forbes Hall, Joseph W. Luter Hall, and Warwick River Residence Hall.

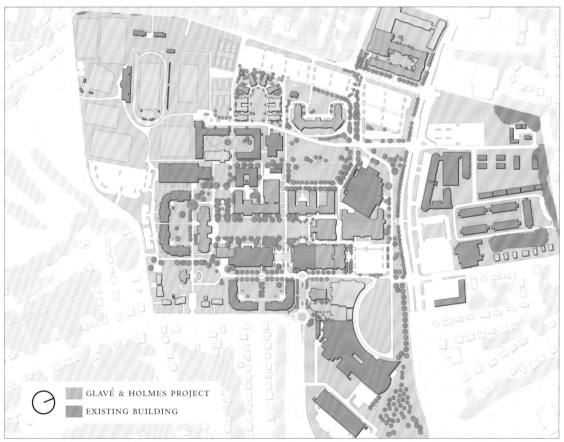

■ GLAVÉ & HOLMES PROJECT
■ EXISTING BUILDING

CHRISTOPHER NEWPORT HALL

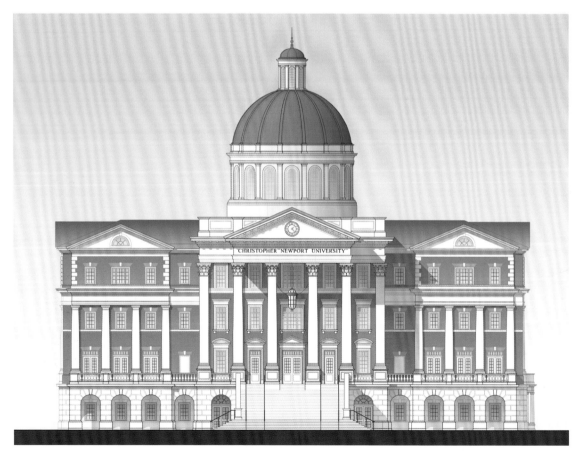

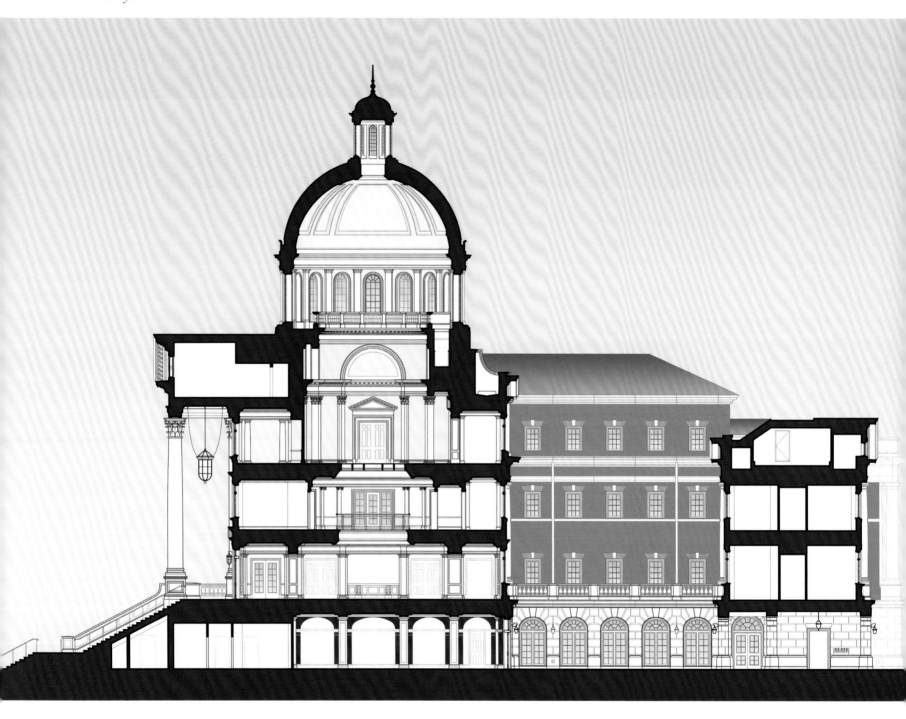

28

LEWIS ARCHER McMURRAN, JR. HALL

OPPOSITE
*Lewis Archer
McMurran, Jr. Hall,
Entry portico
from southwest*

LEFT
Second floor lobby

BELOW LEFT
Entry hall

BELOW RIGHT
Second floor corridor

FREEMAN CENTER

OPPOSITE
*Freeman Center
Expansion, Entrance
from the east*

LEFT
Gaines auditorium

BELOW
Recreational gym

39

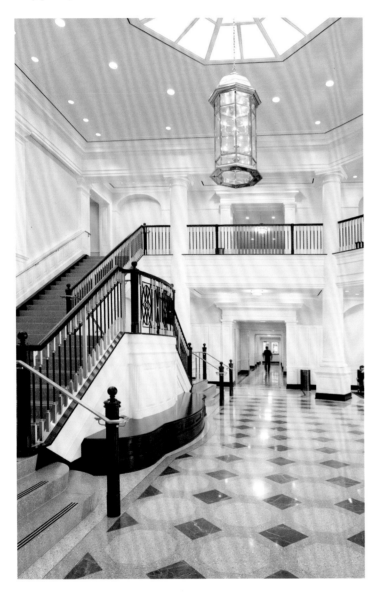

POPE CHAPEL

OPPOSITE
Pope Chapel,
Entrance portico

LEFT
Rotunda lobby

BELOW
Celebration Hall

OVERLEAF
Warwick River
Residence Hall,
View from the
southeast

BELL TOWER

RAPPAHANNOCK RIVER RESIDENCE HALL

GREEK VILLAGE

54

UNIVERSITY OF RICHMOND

— RICHMOND, VIRGINIA —

THE UNIVERSITY OF RICHMOND campus is distinguished by its Gothic Revival architecture, including several early buildings by noted nineteenth-century architect, Ralph Adams Cram. Glavé & Holmes was commissioned to design a new academic facility to house the University's renowned International Studies Program and related fields of study. Sited prominently near the east entrance of the University's idyllic campus, the Carole Weinstein International Center's courtyard and loggias reinforce the established Neo-Gothic architecture of the campus while evoking multi-cultural motifs as they fulfill the requirements of one of the most lauded International Studies programs in the country. The building achieved LEED Gold status and has won several design awards for the firm.

The other Glavé & Holmes University of Richmond project featured here is the Cram-designed, century-old North Court, which was built as a residential community for Westhampton Women's College (now part of the University of Richmond). Long a popular housing option for students, the residence hall was fully renovated, replacing traditional hall-style rooms and common baths with semi-suite configurations. North Court also boasts expanded amenities for social gathering, study groups, and formal meetings. Additionally, the original dining hall and other spaces have been transformed to provide the burgeoning music department with a recital hall, choir room, and premiere practice rooms. Together, these two projects are imbued with the goals of the university to enhance learning and student life in commodious, inspired, energy-efficient, multi-functioning buildings.

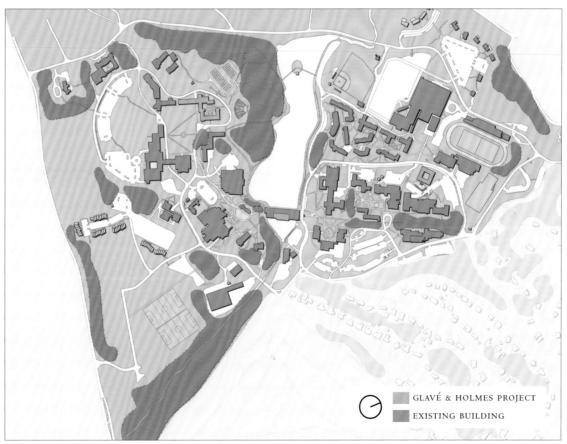

CAROLE WEINSTEIN

CAROLE WEINSTEIN INTERNATIONAL CENTER

NORTH COURT

OPPOSITE
*North Court,
Entrance tower*

LEFT
Courtyard view

BELOW
Double room

OVERLEAF
Perkinson Recital Hall

63

NORTH COURT, PERKINSON RECITAL HALL

UNIVERSITY OF VIRGINIA

— CHARLOTTESVILLE, VIRGINIA —

GLAVÉ & HOLMES ARCHITECTURE and Ayers Saint Gross designed the expansion of University of Virginia's Darden School of Business. The initial phase of the Darden School was designed by Robert A. M. Stern Architects in the 1990s. The more recent expansion phase included designs by Glavé & Holmes for a new parking structure and an Executive Education Residence Hotel addition to Sponsors Hall, the school's hospitality facility. All these additions support UVA's iconic architectural vocabulary, components, and exterior palette. Old Virginia brick, pitched standing metal seam roofs, and window shutters create continuity with the surrounding Darden School buildings.

Glavé & Holmes also designed the renovation of the former Rugby Road apartments into new administrative offices, now called O'Neil Hall. Originally constructed in 1924 for faculty housing, the building (by Fiske Kimball) was a significant example of the Jeffersonian classicism prominent during the early-twentieth century. Glavé & Holmes preserved and restored much of the facility's interior aesthetic including heart pine floors and interior screen doors, while upgrading the mechanical, electrical, and plumbing systems. This project was completed in compliance with Secretary of Interior Standards for Rehabilitation and has achieved LEED Silver certification.

Additionally, Glavé & Holmes served as the Interior Design consultant to John G. Waite Architects on the renovation of UVA's historic 1828 Rotunda. The scope not only included the selection of furniture and fabrics, but also the restoration of existing historic furniture and hand-knotted rugs. Flexible use of both the spaces and furniture are modeled on the innovative Jeffersonian spirit.

OPPOSITE
Darden School of Business, Phase II Expansion, Parking garage arcade views

OVERLEAF
Darden School of Business, Phase II Expansion

DARDEN SCHOOL OF BUSINESS, PHASE II EXPANSION

SMITH

The Inn at Darden

Darden Exchange Bookstore

O'NEIL HALL

OPPOSITE
*O'Neil Hall,
Entry courtyard*

LEFT
Commons corridor

BELOW
Office suite

UNION PRESBYTERIAN SEMINARY
— RICHMOND, VIRGINIA —

GLAVÉ & HOLMES' DESIGNS for the William Smith Morton Library and Allen & Jeannette Early Center for Christian Education & Worship at Union Presbyterian Seminary embody the passion for the preservation and repurposing of buildings espoused by firm founder Jim Glavé. A small campus, Union Presbyterian's Neo-Gothic architecture creates a strong visual identity. The William Smith Morton Library (1996) was created from the shell of Shauffler Hall, a castellated, Gothic-revival former chapel and classroom building, which was designed by Baskervill & Son and built in 1922. Throughout the new library, Christian and literary iconography are incorporated in the design of lamps, carpets, furnishings, and building elements which, together with the dramatic four-story atrium, integrate past and present to create a memorable and welcoming scholastic center for the Seminary.

In 2000, Glavé & Holmes rehabilitated the former library, the 1897 Spence Hall, into a state-of-the-art facility for worship and teaching. The firm left the exterior façade mostly unaltered, while the interior spaces feature a contemporary style with cantilevered floors and moveable walls that offer maximum flexibility. The removal of the old library's self-supporting stacks resulted in a breathtaking volume, which provides respite and calm with light from the existing windows filtering through a mesh scrim.

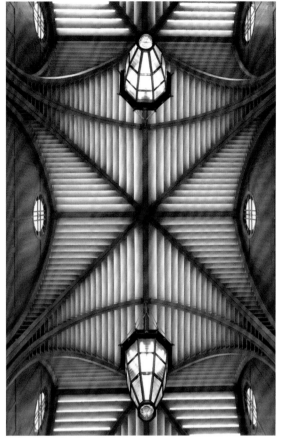

SPENCE LIBRARY
A.D. 1897

1106

OPPOSITE
*Allen & Jeannette
Early Center for
Christian Education
& Worship, Original
library, south entrance*

LEFT
*Contemporary
worship space*

BELOW
*View into classroom
and worship space*

WASHINGTON AND LEE UNIVERSITY

— LEXINGTON, VIRGINIA —

OPPOSITE
Aerial view

OPPOSITE BELOW
*Washington and
Lee University
Campus Plan*

OVERLEAF
*Front elevation of
Washington Hall*

GLAVÉ & HOLMES HAS HAD THE PRIVILEGE of working on numerous projects for Washington and Lee University (W&L). Shown here are the results of the overall plan for the university's historic Colonnade structures and surroundings, the renovation and expansion of Holekamp Hall, and a center for Jewish life.

For the Colonnade—a row of five nineteenth-century buildings at the heart of W&L—Glavé & Holmes led the design for a complete rehabilitation of the buildings, optimizing the collective spaces for offices, including the office of the President and executive staff; classrooms, and an exhibition hall. Likewise, the former dining hall—a c. 1910 Classical Revival building—was transformed into Holekamp Hall, now an academic center for the renowned Williams School of Commerce, Economics, and Politics.

Glavé & Holmes followed the guidelines from the Secretary of the Interior's Standards for Rehabilitation to preserve the major character and defining features in each building while upgrading systems throughout. The interiors were significantly refreshed to become pleasant environments for students, faculty, and staff. As part of the overall Colonnade plan, a below-grade mechanical room was integrated into Stemmons Plaza, incorporating above grade seating and other improvements to the campus landscape. The Colonnade project received both LEED Silver Certification and historic tax credits through the Commonwealth of Virginia's tax credit program.

In addition to its historic renovation work at W&L, Glavé & Holmes created Hillel House, a home for the university's Jewish life. The building is intended to support the cultural identity of Jewish students and community members. The center, designed within the vernacular context of Lexington, includes an adaptable meeting space, library, offices, and a kosher café.

GLAVÉ & HOLMES PROJECT
EXISTING BUILDING

THE COLONNADE

NEWCOMB HALL

OPPOSITE
The Colonnade, Newcomb Hall
collaborative space

ABOVE
Washington Hall exhibit

TOP LEFT
Tucker Hall classroom

TOP RIGHT
Tucker Hall reading room

HOLEKAMP HALL

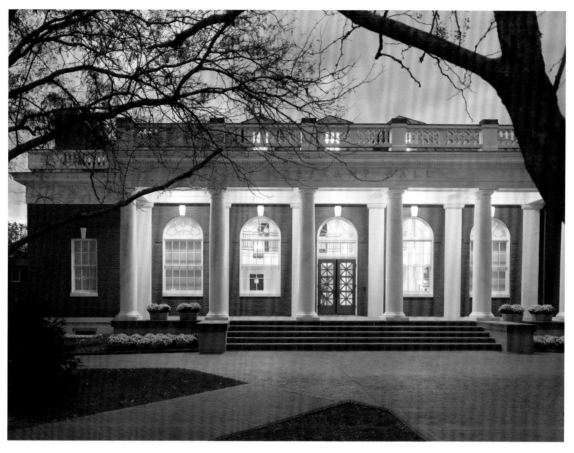

OPPOSITE
*Holekamp Hall,
Entrance
reception hall*

LEFT
Front elevation

BELOW
Gallery view

87

WILLIAM & MARY

— WILLIAMSBURG, VIRGINIA —

OPPOSITE
*Office of Admissions,
View into lobby*

OPPOSITE BELOW
*William & Mary
Campus Plan*

GLAVÉ & HOLMES DESIGNED several projects at William & Mary including the Office of Admissions renovation, the Campus Drive Parking Deck, and the Lake Matoaka Amphitheatre Renovation, all of which have contributed to the physical appearance of the campus, improved services, and promoted enlivened use by the college community.

The Office of Undergraduate Admissions, now housed in the former bookstore building, fulfills its function as the "front door" to the college with a session room for orientations, conference rooms, and administrative offices. The renovation respects the architectural, historical, and cultural context of the college while also effectively communicating that William & Mary is prepared to meet the challenges and expectations of education in the twenty-first century.

Likewise, the Campus Drive Parking Deck is a new structure that accommodates a 500-car garage as well as the college's Campus Police Station and Traffic & Parking Department offices. Glavé & Holmes' design responds to elements found on nearby buildings, integrating both the architectural language of the historic campus and the 1960s-style buildings in the immediate vicinity.

Built in 1947 for Paul Green's drama, "The Common Glory," which depicted the story of Revolutionary-era Williamsburg, the Lake Matoaka Amphitheatre remained a hub of Williamsburg activity until the play ended in 1976. Glavé & Holmes has since restored the Amphitheatre for use by student groups as well as local performers and touring artists. To fully serve the college community, the renovated facility has a new stage, increased seating, a newly raked auditorium, ADA access ramps, underground utilities, a new ticket office, and restrooms.

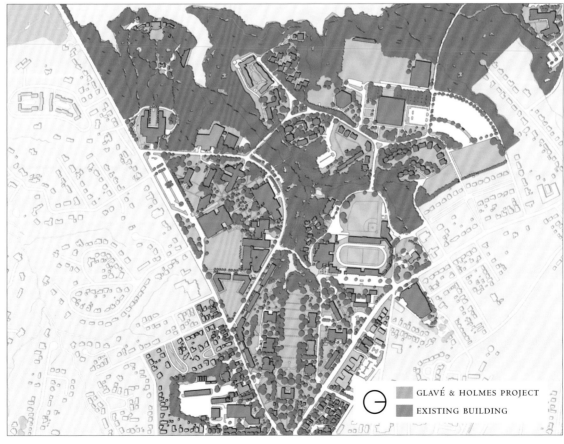

GLAVÉ & HOLMES PROJECT

EXISTING BUILDING

RADFORD UNIVERSITY

— RADFORD, VIRGINIA —

THE 112,000-SQUARE-FOOT College of Business and Economics for Radford University is the result of collaboration between Glavé & Holmes and Ayers Saint Gross. The design supports the college's academic mission and raises the stature of its program among national peers. The building known as Kyle Hall also serves as a gateway to the Radford University campus as it faces both the surrounding neighborhood to the south as well as to the north via expansive glazing that frames the views.

Kyle Hall offers state-of-the-art classrooms and collaborative business school environments, administrative and faculty offices, a two-story atrium, and a flexible assembly space. At the same time, the building reflects Radford's traditional exterior palette of brick, limestone, and slate while expanding the architectural vocabulary towards a contemporary, distilled classicism. The cupola recalls similar features on campus and serves as a marker for the new college. The project has attained LEED Gold status; its sustainable features include green roofs and ice storage HVAC system.

KYLE HALL, COLLEGE OF BUSINESS AND ECONOMICS

RIGHT
*Kyle Hall, College of
Business and
Economics, Exterior
pendant detail*

OPPOSITE
*North elevation,
View from campus*

OPPOSITE BELOW
*South elevation, View
from Tyler Avenue*

RANDOLPH-MACON COLLEGE

— ASHLAND, VIRGINIA —

THE RENOVATION AND EXPANSION of Thomas Branch, a three-story brick residence hall built in the 1920s, was designed by Glavé & Holmes in response to Randolph-Macon's desire to combine existing accommodations for private residential life with new elements supporting student social and academic life. The interior of this building was adapted into student services, offices and seminar space on the first floor and new student residences, now known as the Brock Residence Hall, on the upper two floors. The Brock Residence Hall houses students participating in the Wellness Environment for Living and Learning, one of the new environments currently established on the campus that foster greater connection, collaboration, and community among students.

An existing open courtyard, framed by the three wings of the building, was enclosed to create an atrium to accommodate space for the gathering of students, the interaction of staff members, and for formal receptions. Pre-war buildings on Randolph-Macon's campus inspired the design.

OPPOSITE TOP LEFT
Thomas Branch,
Atrium view
towards balcony

OPPOSITE
TOP RIGHT
Atrium, View
towards entry

OPPOSITE BELOW
View towards new
addition and entrance

ROANOKE COLLEGE

— SALEM, VIRGINIA —

IN RESPONSE TO A GROWING student population on this largely residential campus, Roanoke College requested a new residence hall to be designed and sited in the recently developed athletic quadrangle. Providing an innovative variety of housing options for students, the new facility includes four-bed apartment-style suites and a mix of single and double rooms throughout. This model supports diversity of housing preferences and price points within the same building, gives a student the chance to remain in the same residence hall throughout his or her entire college experience, and encourages transitioning to increasingly private housing from year to year. New Residence Hall also provides an integrated living and learning experience with classrooms, a seminar room, a kitchen, and faculty office space on the lower level.

The exterior design of this new residence hall by Glavé & Holmes is influenced by the existing Collegiate Gothic structures on the campus, featuring rich detailing articulated with brick and cast stone accents. The building is arranged around a courtyard to form a pleasant outdoor space that further enhances residential life. OWPR of Blacksburg, Virginia served as Architect of Record.

VIRGINIA TECH

— BLACKSBURG, VIRGINIA —

GLAVÉ & HOLMES COMPLETED a new 21,690-square-foot combined Visitor & Undergraduate Admissions Center for Virginia Tech that also establishes a welcoming gateway to the campus from the town's Main Street. The new LEED Certified facility is a signature building for the university and serves as an information hub and focal point for both visitors and the academic community. The architecture of the Center combines elements of the traditional Collegiate Gothic with more contemporary interpretations, providing a modern facility that integrates with the campus core. The Center is a two-story building clad in the native limestone that has been historically used on most of the buildings on the Virginia Tech campus. Affectionately called "Hokie Stone," it comes from a university-owned quarry. The building includes a visitor reception area, exhibit gallery, assembly hall, conference rooms, and staff offices. The Visitor Center's gracious reception space presents an exhilarating view of the historic campus through large glazed openings.

OPPOSITE
*Visitor &
Undergraduate
Admissions Center,
View from northwest*

OPPOSITE BELOW
Building entrance

OVERLEAF
*Lobby and
reception desk*

VISITOR & UNDERGRADUATE ADMISSIONS CENTER

CULTURAL INSTITUTIONS
— COLLECTIVE MEMORY, THE DISTILLATION OF CULTURAL VALUES —

CREATING PLACES THAT SET THE STAGE for the preservation, presentation, and promotion of history and the cultural arts has been an important component of Glavé & Holmes' portfolio since the 1960s. Deep interest in history and how it is cared for and passed down through generations began with Jim Glavé. Fifty years later, the firm continues to bring together communities in Richmond, the Commonwealth of Virginia, and beyond, to address the stories of the past. The stewardship of and responsibility for curating history, traditions, and culture is one that the firm holds close.

The Cultural Studio was not as clearly defined when principal Steven Blashfield arrived at the firm in 2009. Nonetheless, Jim Glavé's passion for preserving history established the bedrock for the firm's future. Paramount for Steven and his colleagues is to create places—a vessel—from which stories from the past translate into contemporary discussion. From The City of Richmond's Valentine Museum, which has been a client for over 50 years, to the master plan for George Mason's Gunston Hall, Glavé & Holmes works to connect people and communities with the history that has shaped their context today.

A longtime member of the Virginia Association of Museums, Steven represents the firm in leadership programs for museum administrators, curators, and fundraisers. Museums, in particular, are safe places to have conversations about difficult subjects. Glavé & Holmes' role and understanding goes beyond the architecture and actual building to support this kind of dialogue and inspire curiosity. The Cultural Studio embodies the collective effort necessary to amalgamate public interaction, fundraising, and implementation for both private and state-owned projects. Connection to the public—whether to commemorate a building, landscape, or event, to make accessible collections and artifacts, or to present performances or some combination of the above—is the penultimate goal. A story guides each project to inspire active discovery and retain meaning.

PAUL & PHYLLIS GALANTI
EDUCATION CENTER

— RICHMOND, VIRGINIA —

OPPOSITE
*Paul & Phyllis
Galanti Education
Center at Virginia
War Memorial,
East façade*

OPPOSITE BELOW
*Virginia War
Memorial Site Plan*

OVERLEAF
South façade

THE VIRGINIA WAR MEMORIAL FOUNDATION'S mission is to honor the Commonwealth's heroes fallen in military conflict. The Foundation sought an expansion of the existing memorial complex to accommodate ongoing programming as well as new educational initiatives. Glavé & Holmes designed the resulting 17,300-square-foot Paul & Phyllis Galanti Education Center to be a research center, repository for artifacts, and exhibition space that architecturally compliments the existing Visitor Center and Shrine of Memory.

A place for study and reflection, the new wing of the War Memorial carries forward the language of the existing Shrine building. In order to preserve the prominence of the Shrine, the design put 11,300-square-feet of program below grade, covered by a green roof and plaza at the Shrine level, thereby retaining the open pastoral feeling and view of the James River. The existing palette of fieldstone and beige marble are used on the exterior. A new amphitheater takes advantage of the site's natural topography and panoramic view creating a significant space for outdoor programming.

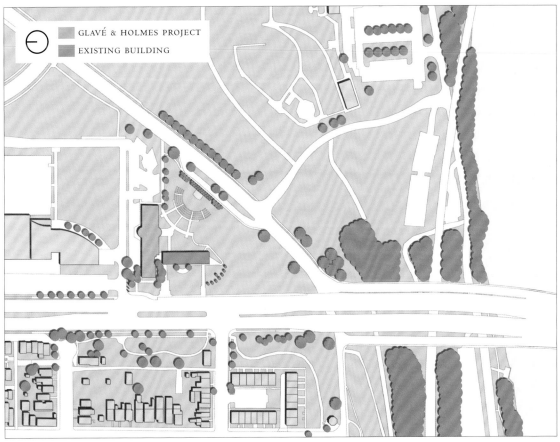

GLAVÉ & HOLMES PROJECT
EXISTING BUILDING

PAUL & PHYLLIS GALANTI EDUCATION CENTER

RIGHT
*Paul & Phyllis
Galanti Education
Center at Virginia
War Memorial,
Exhibit hall*

BELOW
*Entrance lobby
looking towards
Memorial*

OPPOSITE
*Entrance lobby
and reception*

"To be prepared for war is one of the most effective means of preserving peace."

GEN. GEORGE WASHINGTON
First President of the United States
Commander of the Continental Army
Member of the Virginia House of Burgesses

"You never think about yourself. You want to take care of the patients. You want to get them well. I loved them all."

BG Anna Mae V. Hays, USA (Ret.)

"We forgot that our diplomacy could be no stronger than the military muscle we maintained to support it."

"Americans have the right and advantage of being armed — unlike the citizens of other countries whose governments are afraid to trust the people with arms."

James Madison

PAUL & PHYLLIS GALANTI EDUCATION CENTER

THE FABERGÉ AND RUSSIAN DECORATIVE ARTS GALLERIES

— RICHMOND, VIRGINIA —

GLAVÉ & HOLMES' ONGOING RELATIONSHIP with the Virginia Museum of the Fine Arts began in 1995. The firm assisted with renovations for the intimate Fabergé and Russian Decorative Arts galleries, which opened in 2016.

The new galleries—a sequence of five classically detailed rooms that contain the largest Fabergé collection outside of Russia—evolved in collaboration with the Museum's curators, lighting designer, and exhibition design staff to create a technology-rich and awe-inspiring experience for visitors. The centerpiece of this permanent exhibition is a round room created for the magnificent Imperial Easter Eggs, which are displayed in individual cases so that visitors can appreciate their intricacy from all sides.

The design concept for the rooms was inspired by the lavish manner in which such collections were originally displayed. The architecture throughout is meant to echo the character of the precious objects within, and articulates the space with painted columns, cornice, and trim. As the visitor progresses though the galleries, the detail becomes more ornate: from simple wainscoting and cornice in the entry to engaged Doric pilasters and pedestals in the interior rooms. The design culminates with fluted Doric columns and an intricate chair rail in the round room, which also features a shallow, elliptical dome ceiling. The symmetry, simple color palette, and warmth of the stained wood flooring complement and celebrate the exquisite artistry of the collection.

OPPOSITE

The Fabergé and Russian Decorative Arts galleries at the Virginia Museum of Fine Arts

OVERLEAF

The Fabergé and Russian Decorative Arts galleries at the Virginia Museum of Fine Arts

THE FABERGÉ AND RUSSIAN DECORATIVE ARTS GALLERIES

VIRGINIA MUSEUM OF
HISTORY & CULTURE

— RICHMOND, VIRGINIA —

SINCE 1988, GLAVÉ & HOLMES has partnered with The Virginia Museum of History & Culture (VMHC), which was previously known as the Virginia Historical Society. Commissioned to oversee the design for renovations to their existing facility, the firm contributed major additions to the institution in 1991, 2001, and 2006 respectively.

The most recent comprehensive renovation and expansion addressed key goals for the VMHC's newest project: "The Story of Virginia." The museum wished to address developmental issues, its growth and identity, and respond to current trends in museum operations. Glavé & Holmes helped develop a public-friendly prospect by reconsidering the grounds, key outdoor features, and the points of entry and arrival, with focus on the east, south, and west façades. The galleries were reorganized to provide accessibility to a range of patrons and for a variety of museum experiences. The education center was created and the maintenance needs of the building were addressed, including replacement of the mechanical systems in 75 percent of the building.

As a result, the museum can display more of their collections as well as accommodate more and larger special events. "The Story of Virginia" brings the VMHC facility, its collections, and expertise to a wider audience even as the mission—to collect, preserve, and interpret Virginia's past for future generations—remains the same.

VIRGINIA MUSEUM OF HISTORY & CULTURE

THE VALENTINE MUSEUM

— RICHMOND, VIRGINIA —

THE VALENTINE MUSEUM, a local favorite that chronicles the stories and history of Richmond, is comprised of four houses of varying periods—the restored Wickham House, a National Historic Landmark property; the Davis House, the Cecil House, and the Valentine Row House. The Museum sought to renovate and enliven the public spaces on all the first and lower levels. As part of the renovation project, Glavé & Holmes reopened the previously sealed windows on the front of all the houses. The windows reinforce historic provenance, establish a welcoming connection to the street, and have redefined the interiors as well. The public areas—galleries, entry/reception, museum shop, and education areas—were expanded and reorganized to embody the new image of The Valentine. Since the reopening in 2014, the museum has seen an increase in visitation and a rise in frequency of community-centered events.

OPPOSITE
*View of the completed
Valentine Museum*

OPPOSITE BELOW
Courtyard entrance

LEFT
Community Gallery

BELOW
*Permanent gallery
and staircase*

JAMESTOWN SETTLEMENT

— JAMESTOWN, VIRGINIA —

OPPOSITE

*View of the Entry
Pavilion*

OPPOSITE BELOW

*Jamestown Settlement
Site Plan*

IN PREPARATION FOR THE 400TH ANNIVERSARY of the birth of America, the Jamestown-Yorktown Foundation commissioned a master plan to replace the existing 1957 building with a new, larger visitor center, a museum, and an education center. A five-phase plan was envisioned to build each new building on the approximate sites of the originals.

In 1998, Glavé & Holmes was selected to design the Jamestown Visitor Center, Phase II of the master plan, as the gateway and orientation center for the Jamestown Festival Park, the site of the living history museum that celebrates the 1607 founding of Jamestown. The design set up a logical circulation system to link with the future buildings. The 32,000-square-foot facility includes administrative space, ticket and orientation areas, a café, and a gift shop that are organized around a central lobby. A dramatic, two-story wood and glass entry pavilion and its canopy roof supported on structural "trees" recall the natural environment of the original settlement. In 1999, Glavé & Holmes designed the Theater, Exhibition Hall, and Galleries as part of Phase III. For Phase IV, the firm developed space to house 30,000-square-feet of permanent collection galleries. Diaper pattern brick on the pavilions with wattle and daub construction between reinforce a reference to Jacobean architecture, wood-supported canopies over the doorways relate to the wood structure of the Visitor's Center. In collaboration with Gregg Bleam Landscape Architect, Glavé & Holmes designed and completed Phase V, which created outdoor terracing and landscaping throughout the site. The terracing in particular provides ample vantage points from which visitors can experience the historic meadow and tower preserved from the 1957 development.

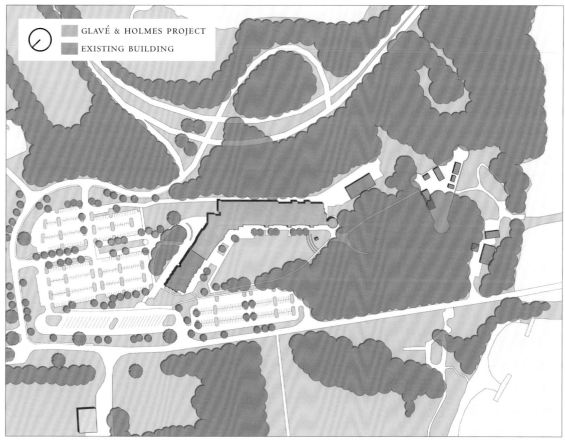

GLAVÉ & HOLMES PROJECT
EXISTING BUILDING

ROBERT V. HATCHER, JR.
Rotunda

JAMESTOWN SETTLEMENT

MORVEN CARRIAGE MUSEUM

— CHARLOTTESVILLE, VIRGINIA —

THE MORVEN CARRIAGE MUSEUM houses a private collection of restored and historically significant European and American horse-drawn carriages. The Glavé & Holmes-designed facility wraps around a smaller existing T-shaped horse barn to create 30,000-square-feet of gallery and flexible mixed-use space for the museum. A cobbled courtyard serves as an outdoor reception area before visitors enter a series of viewing galleries and displays. The interiors feature high ceilings with rusticated classical details and exposed timber trusses, more refined areas for special events, and a balcony for viewing the tops of the tallest and most articulated of the carriages.

The unusual project was inspired by existing historic carriage barns, in particular the Coach Barn at Shelburne Farms in Vermont, and research on the golden age of carriages, which became more of an art form and less utilitarian by the time the automobile came on the rise. To showcase and preserve the collection, special lighting is integrated as well as low volume, humidity controlled mechanical systems, which are zoned independently for each gallery. Wood paneling, bluestone flooring, and the timber trusses create a sense of authenticity appropriate to the content of the museum.

OPPOSITE
View into courtyard

**OPPOSITE
BELOW LEFT**
Main gallery

**OPPOSITE
BELOW RIGHT**
Entertainment pavilion

THE ROBERT H. SMITH CENTER AT MONTALTO

— CHARLOTTESVILLE, VIRGINIA —

OPPOSITE
Entrance porch

OPPOSITE BELOW
New outdoor terrace

OVERLEAF
View from the southwest

DESIGNED IN 1903 as a private residence by Philadelphia architect Charles Barton Keene, Montalto was purchased by the Thomas Jefferson Foundation in 2004. Glavé & Holmes adapted and expanded the house to provide multiple new functions including meeting spaces, teleconferencing center, accommodations for visiting dignitaries, and an event space. The new facility has become the upper campus for the Monticello property; it houses the executive Board Room for the Thomas Jefferson Foundation and is a world-class extension of the Robert H. Smith International Center for Jefferson Studies.

To achieve the ambitious program, Montalto underwent a complete restoration of the exterior and interior and has been enlarged by two sympathetic additions. The front façade, restored to its historic appearance, showcases the distinctive Ludowici tile roof in its original color, restoration of the original stone masonry, and rehabilitation of the original historic windows. An entirely new landscape design by Nelson Byrd Woltz Landscape Architects has been incorporated to provide parking, outdoor terraces, and event spaces that blend into the natural splendor of the hilltop site overlooking Charlottesville. A state-of-the-art catering kitchen avails the center to be used for events, lectures, and weddings. New infrastructure and technology systems, the interior design, and selection of all furniture, fixtures, and equipment complete the scope. The project achieved LEED Silver certification.

THE ROBERT H. SMITH CENTER AT MONTALTO

THE VISITOR CENTER
AT MONTPELIER

— ORANGE COUNTY, VIRGINIA —

GLAVÉ & HOLMES COLLABORATED with Bartzen & Ball to create an elegant and contemporary Visitor Center that is compatible with the scale, forms, and materials of buildings in the surrounding context. Distinctive in its purpose, the Visitor Center at Montpelier is located on the beautiful and original trace leading from Mt. Pleasant to "the Mansion" and greets guests as they arrive to experience the historic home of James and Dolley Madison.

To provide a comprehensive and delightful patron experience, the complex includes a 50-seat orientation theater, gift shop, gallery room, and a café with doors opening to a slate patio. The building interiors, architecture, and landscape design are integrated and contribute to the relationship between the Visitor Center and Montpelier's historic landscape and narrative.

OPPOSITE
*Visitor Center
gift shop*

OVERLEAF
*Visitor Center and
gallery complex*

THE VISITOR CENTER AT MONTPELIER

LEWIS GINTER
BOTANICAL GARDEN

— RICHMOND, VIRGINIA —

LOCATED ON A STUNNING HISTORIC ESTATE, the Lewis Ginter Botanical Garden offers extensive collections and displays of seasonal flowers, grasses, trees and shrubs. Among its commissions there—including the Garden Conservatory, the E. Claiborne Robins Visitor Center, and the Education and Library Complex— Glavé & Holmes imbues the beloved cultural and recreational amenity with its own legacy of public spirit. The E. Claiborne Robins Visitor Center is the gateway and welcome center for the Garden. The structure houses ticketing facilities, meeting and orientation spaces, a garden information area, gift shop, food service and catering, restrooms, and exhibit and office space. Skylights, slate and quarry tile floors, wood latticework, soothing paint colors, floral carpeting, and exterior-style light fixtures all reinforce the garden environment. Glavé & Holmes and Cooper Robertson & Partners collaborated on the realization of this project.

The Education and Library Complex serves as a public resource for continuing education and research in botanical fields. The education center features classroom and laboratory space while the library houses volumes ranging from antique to modern references. The conference center offers a variety of meeting spaces including a 300-seat auditorium.

The Conservatory, the jewel in the campus of buildings and gardens, is comprised of a center mass with a glazed entry portico, classically-inspired steel frame detailing, and a 62-foot-high dome. Three glazed wings extend from the central domed square providing three different climate zones for a variety of plant environments. A large covered terrace overlooking the lake and gardens below is used for events. Glavé & Holmes collaborated with Rough Brothers, conservatory systems designers; Rodney Robinson Landscape Architect; and structural and mechanical engineers experienced in the design and construction of glass houses.

LEWIS GINTER BOTANICAL GARDEN

THE MISSISSIPPI MUSEUM OF ART

— JACKSON, MISSISSIPPI —

GLAVÉ & HOLMES COLLABORATED with Madge Bemiss Architect of Richmond, Virginia and Dale and Associates of Jackson, Mississippi for the design of the Mississippi Museum of Art (MMA).

Crafted from an existing warehouse, the architecturally distinctive result creates a significant new civic arena out of a previously underutilized public space in the City of Jackson. The repurposed building includes new exhibit areas, gift shop, a café, studio school, collections area, and administrative spaces. From jazz programs in the café to performances and presentations in the galleries and the sculpture garden, the MMA attracts people to downtown Jackson and plays a role in its revitalization.

OPPOSITE
New Entrance

OPPOSITE BELOW
Gallery space

ALEXANDER BLACK HOUSE &
CULTURAL CENTER

— BLACKSBURG, VIRGINIA —

OPPOSITE
View from southwest

OPPOSITE BELOW
Front foyer

ALEXANDER BLACK WAS A PROMINENT businessman, founder of the National Bank of Blacksburg, and the grandson of the founder of Blacksburg. To prevent the destruction of his c. 1897 home resulting from development activity on Main Street, the Alexander Black house was acquired by the town in 2002 and moved to its current location. The subsequent Glavé & Holmes restoration and site design converted the Victorian residence into a museum, gallery, and meeting facility. The new center serves to narrate the story of Blacksburg and functions as a community-gathering place.

The firm's general design approach preserved historic fabric wherever possible to retain the building's late-nineteenth-century appearance. Interior reconfiguration of the original core was minimized, historically inappropriate modifications were removed, and a new rear addition was constructed to provide for accessibility and egress to and from the two principal floors. Archival photographs, research, and data were used to determine the historic qualities and original existing materials were utilized where feasible. The Town of Blacksburg successfully merged its resources with a private non-profit foundation to preserve this treasure of local heritage for the community. The resulting project is an excellent example of a public-private partnership.

RESORTS, SPAS, & RESIDENCES

— THE ART OF LEISURE & THE COMFORT OF HOME —

A LONG-TIME MEMBER of the Southern Innkeepers Association, Glavé & Holmes Architecture is known for capturing "the front door moment," a sense of belonging for every guest, while also contributing to the surrounding community in positive ways. Whether a boutique hotel, such as the Dunhill Hotel in Charlotte, North Carolina, or full-scale conference and leisure venues like the Pinehurst Resort or the Hotel Roanoke, the goal—inside and out—is to conjure the historical, cultural, and architectural milieus necessary to create a desirable and lasting effect.

Residential architecture is a natural extension of the firm's polestar value that the visitor or owner experience is at the heart of every commission. Decades of tailoring environments for hospitality projects provide an inherent wealth of experimentation that is distilled to a more intimate scale for families. As with any project, the architect must consider each aspect of the client's experience, but in residential work, every component resonates out of day-to-day necessity. In hospitality, trends are important and are required to be up-to-date and contemporary. With homes, such as those featured here, the architecture and interiors take hold and grow connections over time.

Before arriving at Glavé & Holmes, Randy Holmes' tenure with architect, planner, and educator Jaquelin T. Robertson exposed him to historic houses in Virginia and on Long Island and in particular, the twentieth-century residential architecture of William Lawrence Bottomley. From his formative experiences, Randy believes that the intimate context of residential design deepens both a practitioner's empathy and architectural training. The typology is familiar and the scale is generally manageable, thus providing the chance to learn everything necessary to practice meaningful residential architecture while also preparing a practitioner for a range of scale whether corporate, institutional, or civic.

The love of the client and their aspirations and goals for living—whether as a guest or at home—is at the helm of the Glavé & Holmes creative process. It is leadership's dream for the firm to promulgate the art of the regional house alongside their hospitality projects. Under Randy's direction and complemented by the versatile expertise of the Interiors Studio, opportunities to shape where families and individuals go to retreat, recreate, and live their lives is on the rise. Both the home and the resort provide settings for establishing memories, and in a larger context, supports how individuals participate in society at large.

PINEHURST RESORT

OPPOSITE

*View of Members
Club fireplace after
renovation*

WIDELY KNOWN AS THE "QUEEN OF AMERICAN GOLF," Pinehurst Resort is also a place of quiet repose where guests can reconnect with nature and enjoy the charm of diverse architectural styles found on the grounds. Glavé & Holmes Architecture worked closely with Pinehurst Resort for many years to create and execute an architectural and conceptual master plan that celebrates the resort's turn of the century eclecticism and its storied history.

Founded in 1895 by James Walker Tufts, the original design was created by Frederick Law Olmsted and the Boston architectural firm of Kendall, Taylor, and Stevens. Shown here are Glavé & Holmes' renovated Members Club, 1895 Grille Restaurant and Carolina Dining Room, the Presidential Suite, and the East Wing. The dining and ballrooms overlooking the iconic No. 2 course (by design legend Donald Ross) were unveiled at the 2014 U.S. Open and U.S. Women's Open. Historical veracity is reflected in the new millwork, crafted to complement the originals. New furniture, hand-blocked wallpapers, custom fabrics and carpeting with natural motifs further complement and add to the comfortable, elegant ambiance and update the spaces after years of hard use. The collective renovations inside and out have inspired a flourishing uptick in guest ratings and club membership for those seeking leisure and relaxation in a beautiful and historic context.

OPPOSITE
Pinehurst Resort,
New entrance stair in
Members Club

OPPOSITE BELOW
Lobby of Members Club

BELOW LEFT
Members Club
Restaurant

BELOW RIGHT
Members Club Bar

BEAR IN MIND THAT YOU SHOULD
CONDUCT YOURSELF IN LIFE AS AT A FEAST
EPICTETUS

PINEHURST RESORT

OPPOSITE
*Pinehurst Resort,
East Wing porch at
the Carolina Hotel*

LEFT
*Presidential Suite
bedroom*

BELOW
*Presidential Suite
living room*

159

STONE HOUSE

— PRINCETON, NEW JERSEY —

TAKING CUES FROM the rich architectural heritage of Princeton, Glavé & Holmes served as the associate architect and interior designer for this residence. Built of argillite stone, the house is large in scale, but not grand in its siting and scale of rooms. Numerous intimate spaces were designed for family and friends to enjoy such as the wine cellar, golf room (with simulation of iconic courses), clubroom, loggia with fireplace and terrace fire pit, pool cabana, indoor endless pool conservatory, gym, theater, and two-level library stair-tower. Crafting a cozy and comfortable sensibility in a house of significant size is achieved with attention to proportion, carefully rendered interior details, material palette, and room adjacencies. Glavé & Holmes collaborated with Island Architects, based in Richmond, Virginia and Charleston, South Carolina.

OPPOSITE
Music/living room

OPPOSITE BELOW
Kitchen

OVERLEAF
Entrance court

STONE HOUSE

OPPOSITE
TOP LEFT
Stone House,
Master dressing room

OPPOSITE
TOP RIGHT
Entry detail

OPPOSITE
BELOW LEFT
Entrance hall detail

OPPOSITE
BELOW RIGHT
Dining room

LEFT
Library with
spiral stair

BELOW
Loft library

THE HOTEL ROANOKE &
CONFERENCE CENTER,
CURIO COLLECTION BY HILTON

— ROANOKE, VIRGINIA —

OPPOSITE
*View of new pool
terrace*

OPPOSITE BELOW
*Renovated terrace
outside the Regency
Dining Room*

OVERLEAF
Regency Dining Room

FOUNDED IN 1892, the Hotel Roanoke rises above its namesake city and is intricately intertwined with the region's social and cultural history. Steeped in an ebb and flow of revival and renewal, the hotel has undergone numerous renovations and additions, some prompted by natural disaster or economic trends, and others in response to technological and social changes. The hotel commissioned Glavé & Holmes to provide a continuum with renovations and additions that include guestrooms; The Regency Room, the formal dining room and its adjacent Pine Room; and the pool and pool terrace.

Witness to countless celebrations and imbedded in the memory of many, the Regency Room is as iconic as the Hotel Roanoke itself. Working closely with the hotel and its board of directors, Glavé & Holmes developed a plan that would welcome a new generation of patrons with flexible spaces and upgraded systems, while also maintaining the integrity of the original design. The new Hotel Roanoke pool and terrace also expands the guest experience with a variety of outdoor spaces that function year-round and form part of the pedestrian arrival sequence. No longer an isolated pool area, the renovation—designed in partnership with Four Winds Landscape Design—provides a four-season landscape that reflects the architectural language and materials of the hotel and surrounding Blue Ridge area.

THE HOTEL ROANOKE & CONFERENCE CENTER,
CURIO COLLECTION BY HILTON

OPPOSITE
Hotel Roanoke,
Aerial view of
new pool terrace

LEFT
Pine Room Pub

BELOW
Guest room

CANTERBURY

WILLIAM LAWRENCE BOTTOMLEY originally designed this c. 1930 residence. The property, with a sweeping view of the James River, includes the main house and two flanking pavilions at the west and east of the cobblestone courtyard entry. Glavé & Holmes refurbished the interior of the pavilion and designed an exterior addition to the western pavilion with pool and terraces. Paying homage to Bottomley's established aesthetic, a new veranda, the pool, and garden wall enclosure were added and feature a custom fountain and outdoor fireplace. On the interior, the changing area has a shower with a barrel-vaulted ceiling and a herringbone tile rug centered on the vanity. The kitchen features limed oak custom cabinetry that complements the travertine flooring, which extends onto the pool deck for a homogenous sensibility between the interior and exterior. The successful integration of the new, renovated, and existing architecture enriches the enjoyment of the property for the owner and their visitors.

OPPOSITE
View through pavilion toward pool fountain

OVERLEAF
Pool pavilion looking toward outdoor fireplace

CANTERBURY

RIGHT
*Canterbury, Existing
pool pavilion with new
veranda*

BELOW
*Pool pavilion
sitting room*

OPPOSITE
*Sitting room looking
towards the pool*

OPPOSITE BELOW
*Owner's private
office above
garage pavilion*

THE DUNHILL HOTEL
INTERIOR DESIGN

—— CHARLOTTE, NORTH CAROLINA ——

THE HISTORIC DUNHILL HOTEL, located in the Uptown district of
Charlotte, is the oldest hotel in the city center. Established in 1929,
the hotel was designed by architect Louis Asbury, Sr., and was
originally called the Mayfair Manor. To reinvent the historic, but
outdated hotel as the chicest boutique hotel in Charlotte, the Glavé
& Holmes team crafted a fresh, energetic design that merges Art
Deco and British design elements into a "Cool Britannia" scheme.
The ten-story National Trust Hotel structure is now fully restored
and is a landmark in the arts community and cultural district. The
Dunhill, with its colorful blend of theatricality, trend, and tradition is now a vital part of the city's nightlife and is a favorite
gathering place for those attending concerts, museum openings,
and other Uptown events.

BOAR'S HEAD INN
MEETING PAVILION

— CHARLOTTESVILLE, VIRGINIA —

NESTLED IN THE FOOTHILLS of the Blue Ridge Mountains, Charlottesville's Boar's Head Inn offers guests a luxurious experience in a timeless, pastoral setting. The original Inn, structured around the timbers of an 1834 gristmill, combined both Virginia and English vernacular traditions. The University of Virginia Foundation acquired the Boar's Head in 1988 and commissioned Glavé & Holmes to design a new conference facility. The resulting state-of-the-art Meeting Pavilion expands the Inn's conferencing capabilities with a ballroom, a business center, a breakout meeting room, prefunction space, and a commercial kitchen. The massing and proportion of the building relate to the residential scale of the Inn's context. Like the original structure, the design is influenced by English Arts and Crafts architecture while it embraces regional materials and aesthetic.

BOAR'S HEAD INN MEETING PAVILION

BELOW
*Boar's Head Inn Meeting
Pavilion, Ballroom*

OPPOSITE
*Prefunction
gathering area*

WILLIAMSBURG LODGE AND
THE SPA OF COLONIAL WILLIAMSBURG

— WILLIAMSBURG, VIRGINIA —

GLAVÉ & HOLMES COLLABORATED WITH Culpepper, McAuliffe & Meaders, Inc. to renovate the c. 1938 Colonial Williamsburg Lodge, a structure originally designed by Gilbert Stanley Underwood. Additionally, Glavé & Holmes was commissioned to convert the former Rockefeller Folk Art Museum into a four-star luxury spa and fitness center to serve the Williamsburg Inn and the Williamsburg Lodge. The Lodge project was completed in four phases and the spa was completed as a separate fifth phase, all as part of Colonial Williamsburg Foundation's Master Plan to provide enhanced amenities that serve the needs of tourists and business travelers.

At the Lodge, the historic fabric was retained in the two original buildings while new elements, especially the Conference Center wing and all of the interiors, were contextually designed to respect the existing scale and materials. The Lodge includes 323 guest rooms, lobby, reception, business offices, and a gift shop. The new conference center is fully equipped with ballrooms, conference rooms, banquet facilities, and a full-service restaurant supported by a catering kitchen and back-of-house functions. The restored Lodge entry faces a landscaped arrival court that welcomes guests in a fashion befitting Colonial Williamsburg.

At the spa, the former museum was carefully planned, renovated and expanded to provide men's, women's, and couples treatment areas, lounges, fitness areas, and indoor and outdoor pools. To transform the structures into premiere hotel accommodations and a four-star luxury spa, Glavé & Holmes worked with WTC International Spa Consultants, Mimi Sadler of Sadler & Whitehead Architects, and the Department of Historic Resources.

OPPOSITE
New entrance porch

OPPOSITE BELOW
Arcade looking toward the conference center

188

MILLER CENTER FOR PUBLIC AFFAIRS
PHASES I AND II
— CHARLOTTESVILLE, VIRGINIA —

OPPOSITE

*View into
conference room*

GLAVÉ & HOLMES CREATED THE NEW INTERIOR DESIGN for the University of Virginia's Miller Center for Public Affairs. The project consists of the original c. 1855 central pavilion, known as the Faulkner house, in a classical temple form, and two flanking wings, including the J. Wilson Newman Pavilion designed by Allan Greenberg in 1991.

Historically inspired design schemes were devised. For example, Henry Sargent's "The Tea Party" of 1824 provided the concept for a custom Axminster carpet. Documented period fabrics were chosen and furniture was sourced from historically driven companies. All elements were selected to link the decoration to the mid-nineteenth century. Additional character comes from custom signage, which was based on Sheraton-style chair backs. Historic colors were selected based upon those deemed to work best in a space that is routinely televised. For the reading room, sisal echoes similar floor coverings from nearby Monticello, and crewel and printed linens harken to the casual entertaining grace of porches and loggias in Albemarle County. Enhanced by its exacting and conscious design, the Miller Center has become a vital part of Charlottesville's intellectual culture.

WASHINGTON DUKE
INN & GOLF CLUB

— DURHAM, NORTH CAROLINA —

THE WASHINGTON DUKE INN & GOLF CLUB is a four-star, four-diamond hotel, built on 300 acres in the heartland of North Carolina near the campus of Duke University. Over the years, Glavé & Holmes has completed multiple interior design projects, including the award-winning Fairview and Vista Dining Rooms, the Bull Durham Bar, the Ambassador and Presidential Ballrooms as part of the Conference Center, as well as guest corridors, guest rooms, bathrooms and suites. A beloved facility, the Inn features the Duke University Golf Course, 271 elegantly appointed guest rooms and suites, and superb meeting facilities to accommodate groups from 20 to 600 people.

OPPOSITE
Guest room

OPPOSITE BELOW
Fairview Restaurant

URBAN ARCHITECTURE

— CURATORS OF PLACE, A LEGACY OF PRESERVATION —

A PASSION FOR CITIES AND HOW THEY WORK is written into the DNA of Glavé & Holmes Architecture. Long before the conversion of old warehouses into loft apartments became commonplace, Jim Glavé promoted the salvation of neglected and often historic structures. In the firm's more recent history, Andrew Moore, Director and Founder of the Urban Architecture Studio, has assembled a team of generalists who are drawn to all aspects of the practice of architecture from conceptual design through construction, and who value the patina of history on buildings. Together, studio members seek ways to further a building's story and purpose, or create new buildings to fill gaps in the urban fabric. Above all, whether adaptive reuse, urban infill, renovation, or addition, all projects are skillfully addressed as contextual responses that tangibly contribute to their communities.

The Urban Architecture Studio, in concert with all the firm's studios, maintains and cultivates the responsibility of upholding context. This is the foundation to everything the firm does regardless of the project typology. It is vital to support how people use, occupy, and are drawn to spaces, whether within buildings or the places in between them. Interest in supporting civic fabric, be it in towns, cities, or similar urban/suburban context requires a great deal of creativity—these projects are rich and complex by definition and encompass both large and small-scale interventions.

At Glavé & Holmes there is an expected blurriness between sector/practice areas, which allows for exchange and collaboration. Among the projects that follow, an overwhelming scale is broken down to more approachable pieces such as in the Prince George Parking Garage or College Corner, both in Williamsburg. The Tredegar Iron Works has a new purpose as a Civil War History Center, yet retains elements of its industrial identity. Richmond's CenterStage exemplifies a huge synergetic effort, which entailed repurposing a series of historic downtown buildings into an expansive performing arts complex. The City of Fredericksburg Courthouse remains in the city's downtown core in spite of challenges of a difficult site with numerous physical and regulatory limitations. In these and other urban projects, Glavé & Holmes capitalizes on the essence of a place to develop an appropriate response. Guided by ascendant values of civic duty, social responsibility, and cultural sensitivity, Glavé & Holmes shapes public and private spaces that enhance the public's experience of their cities and towns.

CENTERSTAGE

— RICHMOND, VIRGINIA —

THE CENTERSTAGE FOUNDATION, formerly known as the Virginia Performing Arts Foundation, was created to provide the Richmond area with superior performing arts facilities. Glavé & Holmes was part of a team, along with Wilson Butler Architects, Inc., and BAM Architects, chosen to renovate a series of historic downtown buildings for the envisioned performing arts complex.

The first phase of the project consisted of the renovation and expansion of the historic Carpenter Center. It also included the repurposing of the old Thalhimers department store building into the CenterStage building, which houses the updated 200-seat Gottwald Playhouse, rehearsal spaces, and an education center. The interior of the Thalhimers building was stripped down to its structure and carefully connected to each floor of the renovated Carpenter Center, providing modernized support space and systems for the historic theater. The transformation of both buildings retained historically significant existing features and the original façades.

CHARLOTTE COUNTY COURTHOUSE

— CHARLOTTE COUNTY, VIRGINIA —

SINCE THE EARLY 1800S, the Charlotte Court House district has been the core of Charlotte County's judicial system. Now a designated national historic district, the square includes various historic buildings, including an 1823 courthouse designed by Thomas Jefferson. This structure is the only remaining courthouse designed by the nation's third President.

Following a feasibility study completed by Glavé & Holmes, the County Administration authorized the Circuit Court's request that a new courthouse be built to consolidate the various courts and associated services previously contained in multiple buildings. The new courthouse is sited adjacent to the existing Circuit Court Clerk's Office and across the public square from the Historic Charlotte County Courthouse.

The new 29,000-square-foot structure consists of two above grade floors and one partially below grade level. An enclosed pedestrian walkway connects the new courthouse to the existing Circuit Court Clerk's Office, allowing secure public circulation from one security screening entrance. The courtroom and related spaces are located on grade and upper levels, while the lower level space includes holding cells, the sally port, and secure parking.

OPPOSITE
View of Courthouse entrance from the historic courthouse green

OPPOSITE BELOW
Connector to the existing clerk's office, creating a portal entry from the lower level up to the courthouse green

FREDERICKSBURG COURTHOUSE

THE CITY OF FREDERICKSBURG embarked upon a major planning effort for a new consolidated courts facility to be situated within the city's historic district.

Glavé & Holmes, working with Moseley Architects, provided the design for the exterior of the main courthouse building, which draws from local and historic architecture to be contextually appropriate in downtown Fredericksburg. The scale of the front entry façade draws from the adjacent City Hall and extends its cornice height along the street front. The completed building, with its signature cupola, has four levels and houses the city's Circuit Court and General District Court and their associated support functions. A secure, enclosed parking area is located in the lower level and is accessed from a side street.

CHARLES LUCK DESIGN CENTER

— MANAKIN, VIRGINIA —

As PART OF A COMPLETE TRANSFORMATION of their Architectural Stone Division, Luck Stone Corporation wished to construct a new showroom facility in each of their Stone Division's six locations. The prototype and flagship Design Center, rebranded under the Luck Stone founder's name, was constructed near the company's Manakin, Virginia headquarters. Conceived as an early industrial building that was expanded over time, the Center provides a high-end retail experience within the context of Luck Stone's active quarry and provides a fine balance of refinement and authenticity. The interior of the building, designed as an immersive customer experience with Fraser Design Associates, is embellished throughout with innovative applications of stone. The surrounding site, realized in collaboration with Nelson Byrd Woltz Landscape Architects, includes numerous examples of exterior stone applications, completing the total visitor experience.

OPPOSITE
*View of the Charles
Luck Design Center*

OPPOSITE BELOW
*View of terrace
and gardens*

RIGHT
*Charles Luck Design
Center, Stone
demonstration
terrace*

BELOW
The Studio

OPPOSITE
Entrance

COLLEGE CORNER

OPPOSITE
*College Corner
street façade*

OPPOSITE BELOW
*View from the
northwest*

GLAVÉ & HOLMES WAS ASKED by Colonial Williamsburg Foundation to assist Quinlan & Francis Terry Architects of Dedham, England, to design 35,000-square-feet of new commercial space to complement an important corner in Merchants Square in Colonial Williamsburg. Rubbed and gauged brickwork details combined with precision stone joinery create an exemplary display of architectural craft. Many of the building's unique details were supplied and installed by English master craftsmen. This building is located on Duke of Gloucester Street across from the Kimball Theatre. The new structure provides space for ground floor retail tenants and second floor offices that together enhance the vitality of Merchants Square, drawing more people to the area and extending their visit. The footprint is designed to allow for generous pedestrian circulation around all sides of the site. The wide brick-paved walks, landscaping, and lampposts serve to extend the existing character of Merchants Square around the new building.

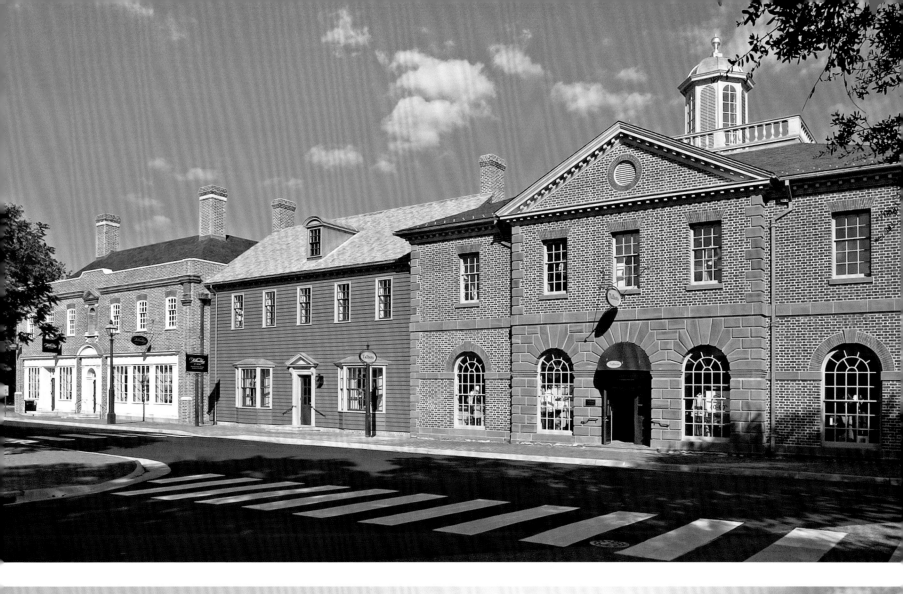

PRINCE GEORGE PARKING GARAGE

— WILLIAMSBURG, VIRGINIA —

GLAVÉ & HOLMES DESIGNED a new 362-car parking garage one block north of Duke of Gloucester Street in Colonial Williamsburg's Merchants Square. Declaring the firm's preliminary designs to be "beautiful and appropriate" for this controversial project, the City Council unanimously approved the Glavé & Holmes proposal.

The success of the parking garage lies in its series of distinct pavilions that provide passersby with the illusion of a much smaller building. Additionally, existing buildings frame attractive views to these pavilions in a manner similar to that of Colonial Williamsburg's historic streetscape. The Prince George Parking Garage was constructed with input from the Colonial Williamsburg Foundation.

OPPOSITE
View of pedestrian entrance from south

OPPOSITE BELOW
View of car entrance

RIVERWALK LANDING

— YORKTOWN, VIRGINIA —

GLAVÉ & HOLMES PARTNERED with Rancorn Wildman Architects and W.M. Jordan Company to create the master plan for Riverwalk Landing, a new commercial center along the York River in historic Yorktown. A key component of the plan is the structural 263-car parking terrace, which was designed to blend with the charming scale of the waterfront houses and new waterfront boutiques. In addition to the contextual design, the parking terrace serves as a gateway from the Colonial Parkway into Historic Yorktown. The parking terrace sits into the hillside to minimize the physical scale of the building and to take advantage of the natural contours, which enable people and cars to access the second level of the deck without an internal ramp. A center open stair connects the upper level to a "town square"—making a pedestrian focused connection between the parking facility and the new retail across the street.

A stair tower at the corner and carefully detailed brickwork help minimize the overall scale of the facility and provide an appropriate backdrop to the village-like setting of Riverwalk Landing's Town Center. A secondary component of the plan includes a small gatehouse that welcomes visitors arriving by boat to Riverwalk Landing. This simple pavilion acts as a lighthouse and gateway for all who come and go to Yorktown by way of watercraft.

TREDEGAR IRONWORKS
AMERICAN CIVIL WAR CENTER
— RICHMOND, VIRGINIA —

THE NATIONAL PARK SERVICE had converted this former ironworks—which provided weapons and ammunition during the Civil War—into a visitor center. The center, however, required access from an arrival and parking area up to the main entrance. Responding to the site's past and its National Historic Register designation, Glavé & Holmes developed the exterior elevator and stair to carefully weave through the ruins while reflecting the machine aesthetic of the setting. Both were crafted of simple steel members painted black to respond to other metalwork on the site.

The elevator was designed to reflect the industrial spirit of the surroundings and clad in glass and steel to permit unobstructed views of the machinery and moving parts inside. Both objects permit visitors to filter through the ruins and have access to the upper and lower levels of the site without compromising any of the historic structures.

OPPOSITE
Exterior elevator and stair from the entry to the Visitor Center

OVERLEAF
Ruins of the former ironworks

ACKNOWLEDGMENTS

Like the design of a good building, the effort to craft a book that captures the collective efforts of a firm over its many years requires the work of many people. For this particular book, its "author" is not a seasoned writer, nor an experienced editor, and therefore I have relied upon many others to help guide and shape this endeavor. I have deep gratitude to my fellow members in our firm's Leadership Team, especially Lori Garrett, Andrew Moore, Steven Blashfield, and Jeanne LeFever, who have supported my desire to document our journey.

Additionally, I am indebted to Crystal Newman-Jones, our Director of Marketing, who has tirelessly assembled images, reviewed, edited and critiqued text, and essentially oversaw the entire process. Without her diligence and patient persistence, this book would never have happened.

I'm also very grateful to so many clients who share our vision for an architecture of contextual compatibility. They partner and labor with us to achieve a refined balance of timeless principles infused with fresh relevance. This book, in many ways, is their testimony.

For the writing and editing, greater credit goes to Henrika Taylor, who has listened well to the stories and heartbeat of who we are as a firm, and sought to coalesce that into a single voice. She, along with Tom Maciag and Dyad Communications shaped the written and graphic layout of this book to express what we wanted to commemorate and document.

We have been encouraged along the way by many in the architectural community; but Calder Loth, Peter Hodson, and Bill Westfall in particular have been crucial guides. From each of them we have received deeper understanding of the systematic elements of our craft as well as appreciation for the rich heritage and architectural legacy handed down over generations.

I would be remiss if I failed to mention my mentor and former employer, Jaquelin T. Robertson, who opened to me the world of great architecture from both the past and present. He was also emphatic about the necessity of design collaboration between the disciplines of architecture, urban design, landscape architecture, interior design, and all the various allied trades and crafts— each a valuable component in making great places and spaces.

This book is dedicated to Jim Glavé, my mentor, advisor, encourager and friend, as well as his former partners, Bill Newman and Pete Anderson, who gave us a strong foundation upon which to build this firm.

My faith is so central to who I am that my acknowledgement would not be complete without expressing deep gratitude to my God and Savior, who has given me the stewardship charge to carry forward his mission through the vehicle of architecture and professional practice. Although I struggle, He loves me still.

To conclude, I owe much more gratitude than words can express to my wife Michaux and my three children, Ben, Drew and Laura. They endured an absent or distracted husband or father throughout the years of practice reflected in this book. Their unflagging support has been the gift that motivates me to continue the pursuit of architecture that elevates the human spirit.

— H.R.H, Jr.

— PROJECT ACKNOWLEDGMENTS —

ACADEMIA

CHRISTOPHER NEWPORT HALL

NEWPORT NEWS, VIRGINIA

Client: Christopher Newport University
Project Principals: Lori Garrett,
   H. Randolph Holmes, Jr.
Project Team: Eleanor Barton, J.B. Elko,
   Lynden Garland, John Glass, Karen Schmid,
   Vanessa Smith, Kevin Svensen
Year Completed: 2015
Photographers: Virginia Hamrick, Ashley Oaks-Clary

LEWIS ARCHER
MCMURRAN, JR. HALL

NEWPORT NEWS, VIRGINIA

Client: Christopher Newport University
Associate Architect: Lord Aeck Sargent
Project Principals: Lori Garrett,
   H. Randolph Holmes, Jr.
Project Team: Eleanor Barton, Lynden Garland,
   John Gass, Gary Inman, Karen Schmid,
   Brandon Sieg
Year Completed: 2009
Photographer: © Prakash Patel

MARY BROCK FORBES HALL

NEWPORT NEWS, VIRGINIA

Client: Christopher Newport University
Associate Architect: Lord Aeck Sargent
Project Principals: Steven Blashfield,
   H. Randolph Holmes, Jr.
Project Team: Eleanor Barton, J.B. Elko,
   Robert Lapinsky, Sebastian Meussling,
   Jaclyn Miller, Lothar Pausewang,
   Karen Schmid, Fernando Viego
Year Completed: 2011
Photographer: Virginia Hamrick

FREEMAN CENTER EXPANSION

NEWPORT NEWS, VIRGINIA

Client: Christopher Newport University
Project Principals: Lori Garrett,
   H. Randolph Holmes, Jr.
Project Team: Eleanor Barton, John Gass,
   Aimee Huber, Megan Johnson,
   Robert Lapinsky, Karen Schmid, Brandon Sieg,
   Fernando Viego, Neil Walls
Year Completed: 2011
Photographer: Virginia Hamrick

JOSEPH W. LUTER HALL,
SCHOOL OF BUSINESS

NEWPORT NEWS, VIRGINIA

Client: Christopher Newport University
Associate Architect: Lord Aeck Sargent
Project Principals: Steven Blashfield,
   H. Randolph Holmes, Jr.
Project Team: Eleanor Barton, Julie Crowe, J.B. Elko,
   Sebastian Meussling, Jaclyn Miller,
   Lothar Pausewang, Karen Schmid, Isolde Uecker
Year Completed: 2013
Photographer: Virginia Hamrick

POPE CHAPEL

NEWPORT NEWS, VIRGINIA

Client: Christopher Newport University
Project Principal: H. Randolph Holmes, Jr.
Project Team: Steven Blashfield, Robert Lapinsky,
   Sebastian Meussling, Jaclyn Miller,
   Kevin Svensen
Year Completed: 2013
Photographer: Virginia Hamrick

WARWICK RIVER RESIDENCE HALL

NEWPORT NEWS, VIRGINIA

Client: Christopher Newport University
Associate Architect: Lord Aeck Sargent
Project Principal: H. Randolph Holmes, Jr.
Project Team: Edwin Holloway, Andrew Moore,
   Robert Parise, Jessica Ritter, Isolde Uecker,
   Jennifer Wimmer
Year Completed: 2012
Photographer: Virginia Hamrick

BELL TOWER

NEWPORT NEWS, VIRGINIA

Client: Christopher Newport University
Project Principals: Lori Garrett,
   H. Randolph Holmes, Jr.
Project Team: Julie Crowe, Kevin Svensen,
   Jennifer Wimmer
Year Completed: 2014
Photographer: Edwin Holloway

RAPPAHANNOCK RIVER
RESIDENCE HALL

NEWPORT NEWS, VIRGINIA

Client: Christopher Newport University
Project Principal: H. Randolph Holmes, Jr.
Project Team: Edwin Holloway, Jaclyn Miller,
   Andrew Moore, Robert Parise, Jessica Ritter,
   Isolde Uecker
Year Completed: 2013
Photographers: Virginia Hamrick,
   The Whiting-Turner Contracting Company
   (Great Lawn Aerial)

GREEK VILLAGE

NEWPORT NEWS, VIRGINIA

Client: Christopher Newport University

Project Principals: Lori Garrett,
    H. Randolph Holmes, Jr.

Project Team: Brian Mork, Robert Riddle,
    Jessica Ritter, Kevin Svensen, Isolde Uecker,
    Neil Walls, Julia Williams

Year Completed: 2016 (Phase I)

Photographer: Virginia Hamrick

GREGORY P. KLICH ALUMNI HOUSE

NEWPORT NEWS, VIRGINIA

Client: Christopher Newport University

Project Principal: H. Randolph Holmes, Jr.

Project Team: Rachel Shelton, Jennifer Wimmer

Year Completed: 2017

Photographers: Virginia Hamrick, Ashley Oaks-Clary

CAROLE WEINSTEIN
INTERNATIONAL CENTER

RICHMOND, VIRGINIA

Client: University of Richmond

Project Principal: Lori Garrett

Project Team: Eleanor Barton, Nickolas Coile,
    Lynden Garland, John Gass, Vanessa Smith

Year Completed: 2010

Photographer: Virginia Hamrick

NORTH COURT

RICHMOND, VIRGINIA

Client: University of Richmond

Project Principals: Lori Garrett, Jill Nolt

Project Team: Lynden Garland, Timothy Hayes,
    Irvin Lynch, III, Jessica Ritter, Rebekah Russell,
    Karen Schmid, Neil Walls

Year Completed: 2017

Photographer: Virginia Hamrick

DARDEN SCHOOL OF BUSINESS,
PHASE II EXPANSION

CHARLOTTESVILLE, VIRGINIA

Client: University of Virginia

Architect of Record: Ayers Saint Gross

Project Principal: H. Randolph Holmes, Jr.

Project Team: Edwin Holloway, Gregory Holzgrefe,
    Jessica Ritter

Year Completed: 2001

Photographer: Virginia Hamrick

O'NEIL HALL

CHARLOTTESVILLE, VIRGINIA

Client: University of Virginia

Project Principal: Lori Garrett

Project Team: Eleanor Barton, Nickolas Coile,
    John Gass, Irvin Lynch, III, Rebekah Russell,
    Vanessa Smith

Year Completed: 2015

Photographer: Virginia Hamrick

ROTUNDA INTERIOR DESIGN

CHARLOTTESVILLE, VIRGINIA

Client: University of Virginia

Architect of Record: John G. Waite Associates

Project Principals: Eleanor Barton, Lori Garrett

Project Team: Mindy Carter Bain, Ashley Long,
    Rebekah Russell

Year Completed: 2016

Photographer: Glenn Suttenfield

WILLIAM SMITH MORTON LIBRARY

RICHMOND, VIRGINIA

Client: Union Presbyterian Seminary

Project Principal: H. Randolph Holmes, Jr.

Project Team: Amy Beatty, Dilip Chakraborty,
    Karen Schmid, John Upton

Year Completed: 1996

Photographer: Maxwell Mackenzie

ALLEN & JEANNETTE EARLY
CENTER FOR CHRISTIAN
EDUCATION & WORSHIP

RICHMOND, VIRGINIA

Client: Union Presbyterian Seminary

Project Principal: H. Randolph Holmes, Jr.

Project Team: Eleanor Barton, James Finch,
    Lothar Pausewang, Vanessa Smith

Year Completed: 2008

Photographer: © Prakash Patel

THE COLONNADE

LEXINGTON, VIRGINIA

Client: Washington and Lee University

Project Principal: Lori Garrett

Project Team: Eleanor Barton, Nickolas Coile,
    Lynden Garland, Veronica Ledford,
    Robert Riddle, Rebekah Russell, Vanessa Smith,
    Winnie Ma Sung, Glenn Suttenfield

Year Completed: 2017

Photographer: Virginia Hamrick

HILLEL HOUSE

LEXINGTON, VIRGINIA

Client: Washington and Lee University

Project Principal: Lori Garrett

Project Team: Eleanor Barton, Edwin Holloway,
    Aimee Huber

Year Completed: 2010

Photographer: Virginia Hamrick

HOLEKAMP HALL

LEXINGTON, VIRGINIA

Client: Washington and Lee University

Project Principals: Lori Garrett,
    H. Randolph Holmes, Jr.

Project Team: Eleanor Barton, Gary Inman,
    Hannah Kim, Glenn Suttenfield

Year Completed: 2007

Photographer: © Prakash Patel

OFFICE OF ADMISSIONS

WILLIAMSBURG, VIRGINIA

Client: William & Mary

Project Principal: H. Randolph Holmes, Jr.

Project Team: Eleanor Barton, Donald Kaupp,
Karen Schmid

Year Completed: 2007

Photographer: Virginia Hamrick

CAMPUS DRIVE PARKING GARAGE AND POLICE OFFICES

WILLIAMSBURG, VIRGINIA

Client: William & Mary

Project Principal: H. Randolph Holmes, Jr.

Project Team: Michael Cook, Lori Garrett,
Donald Kaupp, James Kobus, Karen Schmid

Year Completed: 2006

Photographer: © John Wadsworth

LAKE MATOAKA AMPHITHEATRE

WILLIAMSBURG, VIRGINIA

Client: William & Mary

Project Principals: H. Randolph Holmes, Jr.,
William Hopkins

Project Team: Gregory Holzgrefe, Paul Lucier,
Karen Schmid

Year Completed: 2007

Photographers: Backus Aerial Photography,
Virginia Hamrick

KYLE HALL, COLLEGE OF BUSINESS AND ECONOMICS

RADFORD, VIRGINIA

Client: Radford University

Associate Architect: Ayers Saint Gross

Project Principal: Lori Garrett

Project Team: Julie Crowe, John Gass,
Kevin Svensen, Neil Walls

Year Completed: 2012

Photographer: © Tom Holdsworth

THOMAS BRANCH BUILDING

ASHLAND, VIRGINIA

Client: Randolph-Macon College

Project Principal: James Glavé

Project Team: Edwin Holloway, Gregory Holzgrefe,
Lothar Pausewang, Jessica Ritter,
Jennifer Wimmer

Year Completed: 2005

Photographers: Regula Franz, Thomas Kojsich

NEW RESIDENCE HALL

SALEM, VIRGINIA

Client: Roanoke College

Architect of Record: OWPR, Inc.

Project Principal: H. Randolph Holmes, Jr.

Project Team: Andrew Moore, Robert Parise

Year Completed: 2012

Photographer: Virginia Hamrick

VISITOR & UNDERGRADUATE ADMISSIONS CENTER

BLACKSBURG, VIRGINIA

Client: Virginia Tech

Project Principal: Lori Garrett

Project Team: Eleanor Barton, Andrew Moore,
Vanessa Smith, Jennifer Wimmer

Year Completed: 2011

Photographer: © Joel Lassiter

PAUL & PHYLLIS GALANTI EDUCATION CENTER

RICHMOND, VIRGINIA

Client: Virginia War Memorial Foundation

Project Principal: H. Randolph Holmes, Jr.

Project Team: Eleanor Barton, Steven Blashfield,
Sebastian Meussling, Vanessa Smith,
Melissa Vaughn

Year Completed: 2010

Photographers: Chris Cunningham, © Ansel Olson,

THE FABERGÉ AND RUSSIAN DECORATIVE ARTS GALLERIES

RICHMOND, VIRGINIA

Client: Virginia Museum of Fine Arts

Project Principals: Steven Blashfield,
H. Randolph Holmes, Jr.

Project Team: Eleanor Barton, Jaclyn Miller

Year Completed: 2016

Photographer: Travis Fullerton,
© Virginia Museum of Fine Arts

VIRGINIA MUSEUM OF HISTORY & CULTURE

RICHMOND, VIRGINIA

Client: Virginia Museum of History & Culture

Project Principals: Steven Blashfield, James Glavé,
H. Randolph Holmes, Jr.

Project Team: Henry Ayon, Eleanor Barton,
Amy Beatty, Madge Bemiss, Martha Culpepper,
Ashley Long, Mary Lorino, Sebastian Meussling,
Jaclyn Miller, Ansel Olson, Lothar Pausewang,
Jessica Ritter, Vanessa Smith, William Talley,
Douglas Zirkle

Year Completed: 2015

Photographers: Virginia Hamrick, Maxwell Mackenzie

THE VALENTINE MUSEUM

RICHMOND, VIRGINIA

Client: The Valentine Museum

Project Principals: Steven Blashfield,
   H. Randolph Holmes, Jr.

Project Team: Eleanor Barton, J.B. Elko,
   Veronica Ledford, Sebastian Meussling,
   Fernando Viego

Year Completed: 2014

Photographer: Virginia Hamrick

JAMESTOWN SETTLEMENT

JAMESTOWN, VIRGINIA

Client: Jamestown-Yorktown Foundation

Project Principals: H. Randolph Holmes, Jr.,
   William Lipscomb

Project Team: Martha Culpepper, Edwin Holloway,
   William Hopkins, Morgan Pierce,
   Jessica Ritter, Douglas Zirkle

Year Completed: 2004

Photographers: Maxwell Mackenzie,
   © John Wadsworth

MORVEN CARRIAGE MUSEUM

CHARLOTTESVILLE, VIRGINIA

Client: JWK Properties

Project Principal: H. Randolph Holmes, Jr.

Project Team: Morgan Pierce, Doug Zirkle

Year Completed: 1995

Photographer: © Alan Karchmer

THE ROBERT H. SMITH CENTER AT MONTALTO

CHARLOTTESVILLE, VIRGINIA

Client: Thomas Jefferson Foundation

Project Principal: H. Randolph Holmes, Jr.

Project Team: Steven Blashfield, Gary Inman,
   Veronica Ledford, Greta Van Tiem

Year Completed: 2011

Photographers: Virginia Hamrick, © Ansel Olson

THE VISITOR CENTER AT MONTPELIER

ORANGE COUNTY, VIRGINIA

Client: Montpelier Foundation

Associate Architect: Bartzen & Ball Architects

Project Principals: Madge Bemiss,
   H. Randolph Holmes, Jr.

Project Team: James Finch, Gregory Holzgrefe,
   Sebastian Meussling, Robert Parise,
   Lothar Pausewang

Year Completed: 2006

Photographer: Maxwell Mackenzie

LEWIS GINTER BOTANICAL GARDEN

RICHMOND, VIRGINIA

Client: Lewis Ginter Botanical Garden

Associate Architect: Cooper Robertson & Partners
   Architects (Visitor Center)

Project Principal: H. Randolph Holmes, Jr.

Project Team: Amy Beatty, Madge Bemiss,
   Martha Culpepper, Beth Fowler, Peter Fraser,
   Donald Kaupp, S. Jeanne LeFever, Mary Lorino,
   Lothar Pausewang, Jennifer Reid, Jessica Ritter,
   Karen Schmid

Year Completed: 2002

Photographers: Robert Chancler (Visitor Center),
   Blaine Harrington, III (Education Building),
   © John Wadsworth (Conservatory)

THE MISSISSIPPI MUSEUM OF ART

JACKSON, MISSISSIPPI

Client: Mississippi Museum of Art

Associate Architects: Madge Bemiss Architect,
   Dale & Associates Architects

Project Principal: Madge Bemiss

Project Team: James Finch, Sebastian Meussling

Year Completed: 2007

Photographer: Greg Campbell

ALEXANDER BLACK HOUSE & CULTURAL CENTER

BLACKSBURG, VIRGINIA

Client: Town of Blacksburg

Project Principals: Steven Blashfield,
   H. Randolph Holmes, Jr.

Project Team: Vanessa Smith, Greta Van Tiem,
   Fernando Viego

Year Completed: 2014

Photographer: © Ansel Olson

PINEHURST RESORT

VILLAGE OF PINEHURST, NORTH CAROLINA

Client: Pinehurst Resort

Project Principals: H. Randolph Holmes, Jr.,
 Gary Inman

Project Team: Eleanor Barton, Julie Crowe,
 Leah Embrey, Kalee Hartman, Veronica Ledford,
 Robert Parise, Shawna Schmidt, Kathy Thomas,
 Jennifer Wimmer

Year Completed: Ongoing at date of publication.

Photographers: Kip Dawkins, © Ansel Olson,
 Tim Sayer

STONE HOUSE

PRINCETON, NEW JERSEY

Client: Private

Architect of Record: Wallace Architects, Inc.

Project Principals: H. Randolph Holmes, Jr.,
 Gary Inman

Project Team: Eleanor Barton, Mindy Carter Bain,
 J.B. Elko, Veronica Ledford, Jennifer Rhoades

Year Completed: 2012

Photographer: © Ansel Olson

THE HOTEL ROANOKE & CONFERENCE CENTER, CURIO COLLECTION BY HILTON

ROANOKE, VIRGINIA

Client: Hotel Roanoke & Conference Center

Project Principal: Gary Inman

Project Team: Vanessa Smith

Year Completed: Ongoing at date of publication.

Photographers: © Ansel Olson, Glenn Suttenfield

CANTERBURY

RICHMOND, VIRGINIA

Client: Private

Project Principal: H. Randolph Holmes, Jr.,

Project Team: Mindy Carter Bain, Leah Embrey,
 Kalee Hartman, Jennifer Wimmer

Year Completed: 2017

Photographer: Glenn Suttenfield

THE DUNHILL HOTEL INTERIOR DESIGN

CHARLOTTE, NORTH CAROLINA

Client: Summit Hospitality Group

Project Principal: Gary Inman

Project Team: Shawna Schmidt

Year Completed: 2015

Photographer: Kip Dawkins

BOAR'S HEAD INN MEETING PAVILION

CHARLOTTESVILLE, VIRGINIA

Client: University of Virginia Foundation

Project Principal: H. Randolph Holmes, Jr.

Project Team: Julie Crowe, Jaclyn Miller,
 Robert Parise, Karen Schmid

Year Completed: 2009

Photographer: © Ansel Olson

WILLIAMSBURG LODGE

WILLIAMSBURG, VIRGINIA

Client: Colonial Williamsburg Foundation

Architect of Record: Culpepper, McAuliffe &
 Meaders, Inc.

Project Principal: H. Randolph Holmes, Jr.

Project Team: William Hopkins, Robert Parise,
 Jennifer Wimmer, Douglas Zirkle

Year Completed: 2006

Photographer: © Eric Taylor

THE SPA OF COLONIAL WILLIAMSBURG

WILLIAMSBURG, VIRGINIA

Client: Colonial Williamsburg Foundation

Project Principal: H. Randolph Holmes, Jr.

Project Team: Madge Bemiss, James Finch,
 Lothar Pausewang, Jennifer Wimmer

Year Completed: 2007

Photographer: Chris Cunningham

MILLER CENTER FOR PUBLIC AFFAIRS, PHASES I AND II

CHARLOTTESVILLE, VIRGINIA

Client: University of Virginia

Project Principal: Gary Inman

Project Team: Eleanor Barton, Mindy Carter Bain,
 Vanessa Smith

Year Completed: 2012

Photographer: © Ansel Olson

WASHINGTON DUKE INN & GOLF CLUB

DURHAM, NORTH CAROLINA

Client: Washington Duke Inn & Golf Club

Project Principal: Gary Inman

Project Team: J.B. Elko, Veronica Ledford,
 Jessica Ritter, Catherine Stanley,
 Jennifer Wimmer

Year Completed: Ongoing at date of publication.

Photographer: © Washington Duke Inn & Golf Club

CENTERSTAGE

RICHMOND, VIRGINIA

Client: Virginia Performing Arts Foundation
Architect of Record: Wilson Butler Architects
Associate Architect: BAM Architects
Project Team: Robert Parise
Year Completed: 2000
Photographer: © Robert Benson Photography

CHARLOTTE COUNTY COURTHOUSE

CHARLOTTE COUNTY, VIRGINIA

Client: Charlotte County
Project Principals: H. Randolph Holmes, Jr.,
   Andrew Moore
Project Team: Eleanor Barton, Aaron Chupp,
   Kate Hershey
Year Completed: 2018
Photographer: Lee Brauer

FREDERICKSBURG COURTHOUSE

FREDERICKSBURG, VIRGINIA

Client: City of Fredericksburg
PPEA Partners: Moseley Architects,
   English Construction
Project Principal: H. Randolph Holmes, Jr.
Project Team: Edwin Holloway, Jaclyn Miller,
   Andrew Moore
Year Completed: 2014
Photographer: Lee Brauer

CHARLES LUCK DESIGN CENTER

MANAKIN, VIRGINIA

Client: Luck Stone Corporation
Project Team: Edwin Holloway, Andrew Moore,
   Brandon Sieg, Douglas Zirkle
Year Completed: 2007
Photographers: Chris Cunningham, Todd Wright

COLLEGE CORNER

WILLIAMSBURG, VIRGINIA

Client: Colonial Williamsburg Foundation
Architect of Record: Quinlan Terry Architects
Project Principal: H. Randolph Holmes, Jr.
Project Team: William Hopkins, Jessica Ritter,
   Douglas Zirkle
Year Completed: 2004
Photographer: © John Wadsworth

PRINCE GEORGE PARKING GARAGE

WILLIAMSBURG, VIRGINIA

Client: City of Williamsburg
Project Principals: H. Randolph Holmes, Jr.,
   William Lipscomb
Project Team: Michael Cook, Morgan Pierce,
   Jessica Ritter, Karen Schmid
Year Completed: 2004
Photographer: © John Wadsworth

RIVERWALK LANDING

YORKTOWN, VIRGINIA

Client: York County
Joint Venture: Rancorn Wildman Architects
Project Principal: H. Randolph Holmes, Jr.
Project Team: Donald Kaupp
Year Completed: 2005
Photographer: Chris Cunningham

TREDEGAR IRONWORKS AMERICAN CIVIL WAR CENTER

RICHMOND, VIRGINIA

Client: Richmond Riverfront
   Development Corporation
Project Principals: James Glavé, William Lipscomb
Project Team: Morgan Pierce
Year Completed: 2000
Photographer: © Ansel Olson

N.B. Every effort has been made to make the project acknowledgments accurate as of this printing. If there is any omission, it is unintentional. Please contact Glavé & Holmes to correct their archival files.

"*More than ever, we need places of Beauty*
that allow for the best of human progress to flourish...
Places that challenge us to see ourselves
not as who we are, but who we can become."

—

H. RANDOLPH HOLMES, JR.

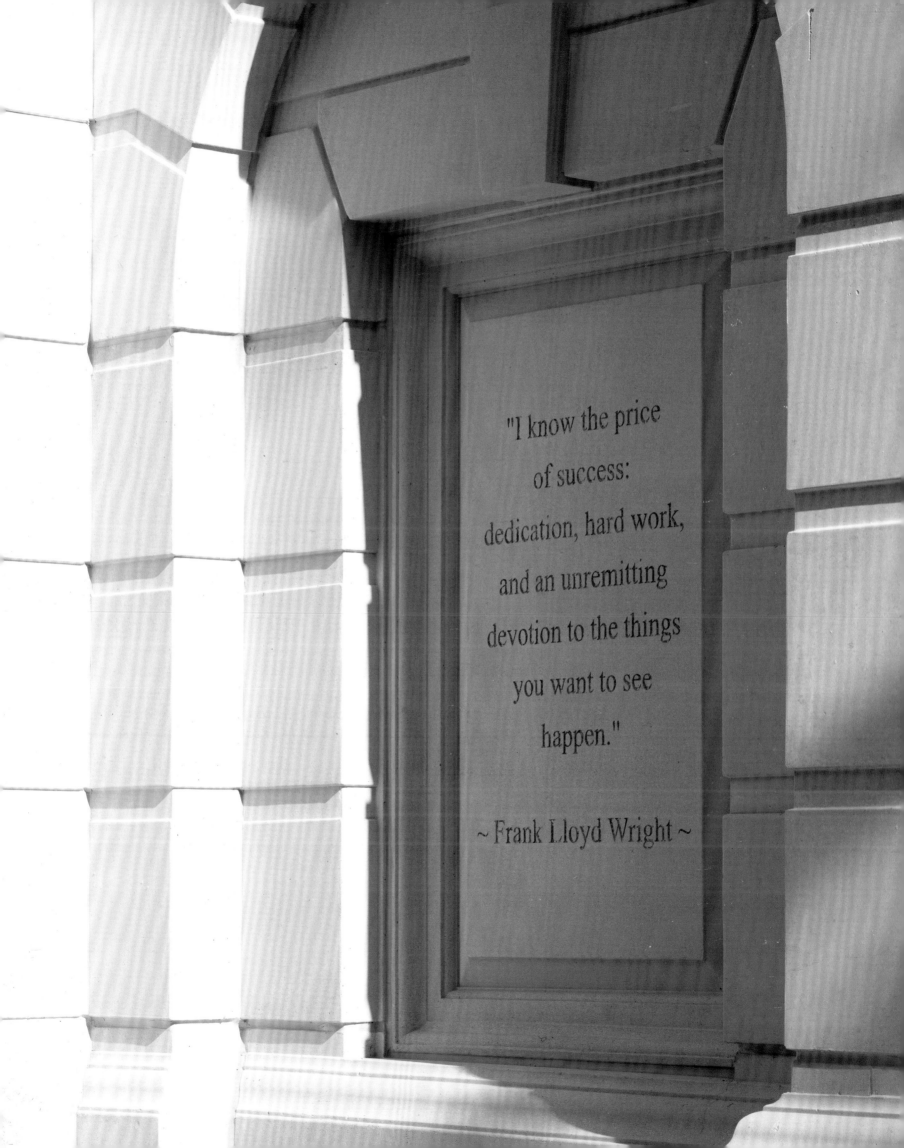

"I know the price
of success:
dedication, hard work,
and an unremitting
devotion to the things
you want to see
happen."

~ Frank Lloyd Wright ~

CONTACT

2101 East Main Street, Richmond, Virginia 23223

ISBN 978-0-578-48047-3
LIBRARY OF CONGRESS CONTROL NUMBER 2019910767
FIRST EDITION

WRITER

H. Randolph Holmes, Jr. with Henrika Dyck Taylor

EDITORIAL

Crystal Newman-Jones, Henrika Dyck Taylor

DESIGNER

Dyad Communications
Philadelphia, Pennsylvania

PRINTER

Printed in China

FRONT JACKET IMAGE: Front entrance to Christopher Newport Hall at Christopher Newport University. Photography by Ashley Oaks-Clary.

BACK COVER IMAGE: Exterior light fixture detail at Kyle Hall at Radford University. Photography by © Tom Holdsworth.

ENDPAPERS: Drawing of the Central Dome at Lewis Ginter Botanical Garden by Lothar Pausewang.

OPPOSITE TITLE PAGE: Christopher Newport Hall at Christopher Newport University. Photography by Virginia Hamrick.

OPPOSITE TABLE OF CONTENTS: Map of Richmond. Unknown provenance.

PAGE 18: Pope Chapel at Christopher Newport University. Photography by Virginia Hamrick.

AUTHOR, GROUP, AND PAGE 15 PHOTOGRAPHY: Peter Olson

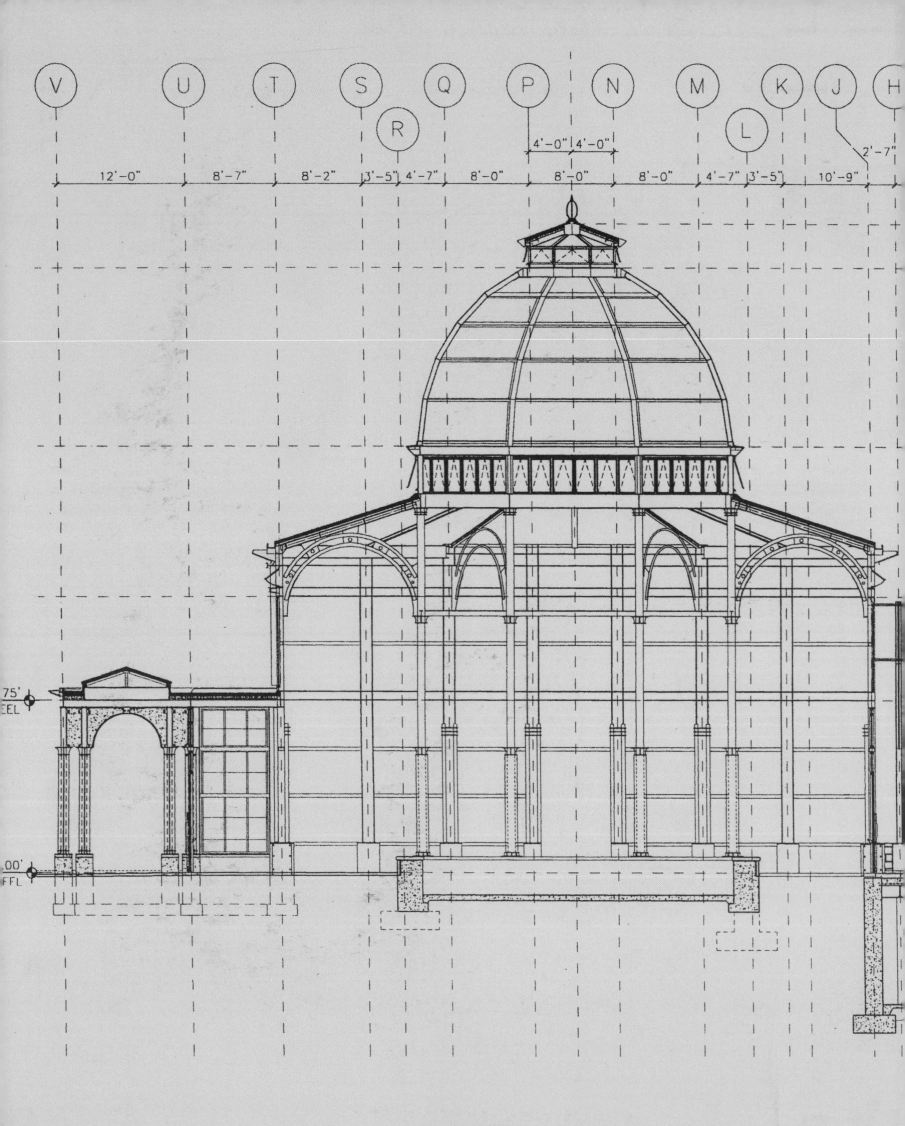